Save The World
Before Breakfast

An Introduction to
Design-Driven Entrepreneurship

Niloufar Gharavi

Save The World Before Breakfast

An Introduction to Design-Driven Entrepreneurship

Niloufar Gharavi

November 2025

Others have seen what is and asked why.
I have seen what could be and asked why not.

—Pablo Picasso

Published by Evolutesix Books, London, UK.

Paperback ISBN: 978-1-913629-22-9

Hardback ISBN: 978-1-913629-21-2

e-book ISBN: 978-1-913629-23-6

Copyright © Niloufar Gharavi, November 2025

The rights of Niloufar Gharavi to be identified as
the author of this work has been asserted by her in accordance
with the Copyright, Designs and Patents Act 1988.

A CIP catalogue record will be available from the British Library.

Cover and Graphics by Behnam Emami

Collaborative Edit by Mohebat Rezvani

To my family, who taught me that building isn't just a job, it's a way of life.

And to all entrepreneurs out there doing the same, quietly shaping a better world for everyone.

To those who never quite fit in, yet belong everywhere.

To the ones who move between worlds, holding them together in ways no one sees.

Table of Content

Brief Intro .... Page 6

Chapter 1: Being an Entrepreneur .... Page 15

Chapter 2: The Multiverse of Making .... Page 37

Chapter 3: Building by Design .... Page 55

Chapter 4: Tea, Wine and Trust .... Page 73

Chapter 5: Dancing with the System .... Page 83

Chapter 6: Inventing Beyond the Obvious .... Page 103

Chapter 7: Building from Scratch .... Page 111

Chapter 8: The Real Help Entrepreneurs Need .... Page 127

Chapter 9: Design in the "Wilderness" .... Page 141

Chapter 10: Bias, Barriers, and Bridges .... Page 159

Chapter 11: Designing Teams that Innovate .... Page 173

Chapter 12: Imagining the Unknown .... Page 191

Ending .... Page 198

Bibliography .... Page 202

Brief Intro

There's a certain magic in the early morning hours, when the world is quiet, and the possibilities seem endless. Before the emails start pinging, before the to-do lists take over, there's a fleeting moment when the mind is free to wander, to imagine, to solve. It's in this sliver of time that the most audacious ideas are born, the ones that make your heart race just a little faster. A moment so profound that it almost feels like, maybe, and only maybe, you're about to "save the world before breakfast."

But this isn't about chasing unicorn myths or superhero fantasies, it's about something far more real, deeply humbling, and quietly revolutionary. Capturing that raw, unfiltered vision before the weight of reality has a chance to crush it. It's about believing, if only for a few minutes, that we really can reimagine systems, redesign broken processes, and rebuild what's been lost. It's the courage to act on ideas before practicality and self-doubt creep in.

This book is about that moment, about turning sparks of inspiration into strategies, blueprints, and ventures that can thrive in the real world.

It's about harnessing the designer's mindset to see problems from new angles, the entrepreneur's grit to build something from nothing, and the systemic thinker's vision to scale it all sustainably.

To save the world before breakfast is to challenge assumptions before they harden, to act quickly and think expansively.

It's a mindset that embraces curiosity, optimism, and the relentless pursuit of better ways to do things, whether that's redesigning a simple cup or reimagining entire industries.

So, as you turn these pages, I invite you to lean into that morning mindset, to see not just what is, but what could be. After all, if we're going to save the world, why wait until after breakfast?

Entrepreneurship is the quiet courage of those who keep going, like the street vendor in Jakarta reinventing her business after a flood wiped out her stall, the 17-year-old coder in Dhaka launching a social impact app from his bedroom, or the retired farmer in rural Sweden transforming her land into a regenerative food hub. It lives wherever someone chooses to act on a need, despite uncertainty.

And yet, in today's world, that courage needs to scale. Because businesses don't operate in silos, they exist within complex, interconnected ecosystems. The climate crisis, global inequality, and fragmented industries aren't challenges that can be solved with a single product or an overnight IPO. They demand something more: not just bold individuals, but bold systems. Systems designed for collaboration, resilience, and long-term impact.

I didn't learn this from books alone. I learned it through my own journey, from growing up in a family of serial entrepreneurs to studying architecture, design and business, from navigating industries dominated by legacy thinking to founding my own ventures, from Iran to Norway, and now, globally.

This book isn't just about entrepreneurship. It's about Design-Driven Entrepreneurship (DDE), a way of thinking that blends creativity, business strategy, and systemic problem-solving into one powerful approach. This book, through the introduction of Design-Driven Entrepreneurship (DDE), challenges the current ways innovation is nurtured and practiced, urging us to rethink how ideas are brought to life. It doesn't just propose new methods—it invites a shift in mindset, where creativity, empathy, and systems thinking replace outdated formulas for progress.

But more than that, this book is a story.

It's a story of resilience. Of questioning everything you thought you knew. Of waking up with an idea so powerful it keeps you up at night. It's about standing at the edge of uncertainty, knowing you might fail, but still choosing to step forward.

It's my story, but it's also the story of every entrepreneur, designer, and changemaker who refuses to accept the world as it is and dares to reimagine what it could be.

The Journey Behind This Book

Growing up in Iran, I was surrounded by entrepreneurs, engineers, and social innovators. My father built industrial factories and pioneered construction systems, while my mother created educational institutions and social enterprises that changed lives. The conversations at our dinner table weren't just about what happened that day, they were about the next big idea, the next challenge, the next impossible thing that needed to be done.

That foundation led me to architecture, then to systemic design, and eventually into the world of startups. But something always felt missing.

I saw brilliant entrepreneurs struggling to turn their visions into scalable businesses, not because their ideas weren't good, but because they were approaching the process with the wrong mindset.

I saw startups chasing growth at all costs, ignoring the systems they were operating within, and ultimately failing because they couldn't adapt.

I saw businesses focusing on short-term wins instead of long-term impact, leading to solutions that barely scratched the surface of the real problems they were meant to solve.

And through it all, I saw one common theme: a lack of design-driven thinking.

Why Design?

Design is more than aesthetics or functionality. It's a mindset, a way of thinking critically, exploring possibilities, and shaping solutions that are human-centered, system-conscious, and future-ready.

To think like a designer is to:
- Challenge the status quo – Designers don't settle for "how it's always been done." They ask bold questions like "What if?" and "Why not?"
- Embrace uncertainty – While traditional business thinking leans on rigid plans, designers are comfortable navigating ambiguity and complexity.

- Prototype and iterate – Instead of chasing perfection, designers build quickly, test early, and refine often, treating failure as feedback.
- Zoom out and connect the dots – Design thinking considers the broader system. A product or service is never isolated; it lives within a larger social, economic, and environmental context.
- Design for real people – At the heart of every meaningful solution is empathy, a deep understanding of human needs, behaviors, and desires.

When applied to entrepreneurship, design becomes a powerful advantage. It enables founders to:

- Build ventures that solve real, validated problems.
- Avoid common traps like premature scaling or misaligned market fit.
- Develop adaptive, resilient solutions that grow with changing needs.
- Transform constraints into catalysts for innovation.

In a world where complexity is the norm, design equips entrepreneurs not just to survive, but to lead with purpose and clarity.

Find 50 New Ways To Drink Water

Design schools are all about breaking assumptions, embracing chaos, and exploring possibilities that no one else see.

I'll never forget one of my first design exercises at school: "Find 50 new ways to drink water."

At first, it felt ridiculous. A glass, a bottle, a tap, what else could there be? But as I started brainstorming, I realized this was more than just a silly exercise. It was about stretching my thinking beyond the obvious.

One classmate imagined drinking it as vapor, inhaled like mist.

Another thought about absorbing it through the skin, like a plant.

Someone else suggested turning it into edible pearls, bursting with flavor.

And suddenly, I saw the world differently. Every problem became an open-ended question. Every assumption could be challenged.

That's the mindset that entrepreneurs need.

Because when you look at the business world today, you'll see that the most groundbreaking companies weren't built by following the rules. They were built by people who questioned everything and dared to design something better.

Airbnb asked: Why do people need hotels? What if homes could be turned into hospitality experiences?

Netflix asked: What if people didn't have to follow TV schedules? What if the entire world of entertainment could be on-demand?

Apple asked: What if computers weren't just tools, but beautifully designed experiences?

The best entrepreneurs don't just start businesses, they design them.

What You'll Learn In This Book

- Why traditional startup models fail, and how to fix them
- The power of systemic thinking in solving complex challenges
- How to design for impact and profitability at the same time
- Real-world case studies of startups that succeeded (and failed) because of design
- Practical exercises to help you think like a designer and apply Design-Driven Entrepreneurship (DDE) to your work

This book is part storytelling, part strategy, and part hands-on guide. It's meant to challenge you, inspire you, and give you practical tools to create a business that thrives in complexity.

Who Is This Book For?

- Entrepreneurs who want to build businesses that stand out and scale effectively.
- Designers who want to expand their impact beyond aesthetics and into business innovation.
- Investors looking for smarter ways to evaluate startups and identify winners,

- Leaders & Changemakers who see challenges and want to design meaningful solutions.
- Anyone who's tired of the same old startup playbook, and is ready for something new.

If you've ever looked at the world and thought, "There has to be a better way," this book is for you.

If you believe business can be more than just profit, it can be a force for good, a tool for impact, a way to shape the future, then let's challenge the status quo.

Kindly,
Nilu

Chapter 1:
Being an Entrepreneur

Entrepreneurship, as I've come to understand it, is a relentless pursuit of resilience and determination. Whether it's a single mother in Bogotá financing her children's education by selling Christmas hats on the streets, or a media-star tech entrepreneur generating billions of dollars in Silicon Valley, the essence of entrepreneurship is about getting knocked down a hundred times and finding the strength to get back up, just one more time. It's about facing challenges head-on and refusing to yield in the face of adversity.

How did I get to learn this? Let me tell you a story about my family.

We are Iranians, descendants of ancient Persia, residing in a land rich in history and resources. Iran, cradled between Afghanistan and Iraq, is a country that boasts a strategic position, with the Caspian Sea to its north and the Persian Gulf and Gulf of Oman to its south.

This nation, stretching over 1.6 million square kilometers[1], is more than just a geopolitical entity on the world map; it's a melting pot of cultures, ideas, and histories. Home to over 90 million people[2], Iran is a tapestry of diverse ethnicities and languages, each contributing to the country's rich cultural fabric. From the bustling streets of Tehran to the majestic ruins of Persepolis, Iran's landscape is as varied as its history.

Iran's modern history is particularly compelling, marked by significant events that have shaped its current identity. Understanding Iran's journey, especially through the lens of these historical events, is crucial to grasping the context in which my family's story unfolds, forming the roots of my approach to design-driven entrepreneurship.

Iran's journey is a narrative deeply intertwined with the nation's highs and lows, reflecting the resilience and adaptability inherent in the Iranian spirit. Growing up in such a context, my approach to design and entrepreneurship is as much about innovative thinking, creative problem-solving, and impactful business as it is about navigating the complexities of an ever-changing world.

So, bear with me just for a moment as I share a brief history of Iran, so you can understand the context of my story better.

The Islamic Revolution of 1979[3] was a turning point, drastically altering the nation's trajectory. This revolution, a complex interplay of political, religious, and social factors, brought about profound changes in Iran's governance and society.

Prior to the revolution, Iran was under the rule of Mohammad Reza Shah Pahlavi. The Shah's reign, which began in 1941, was marked by a strong push towards modernization and Westernization. His policies, heavily influenced by Western ideals, aimed at transforming Iran into a global power, often at the expense of traditional and religious values.

This period saw rapid urbanization, the growth of education, and the advancement of women's rights. However, as history would tell the tale, society was far from ready to embrace these rapid changes.

The tipping point came in 1978 when widespread demonstrations and civil resistance began to shake the foundations of the Shah's rule. The protests, initially focused on political freedom and economic woes, gradually coalesced into a revolution with the overarching aim of establishing an Islamic state. The Shah's attempts to quell the unrest only intensified the public's determination.

In January 1979, the Shah left Iran, a move that signaled the end of his regime, and the Islamic Republic of Iran was established shortly after that. This new government, rooted in Shia Islam, represented a dramatic shift from the Shah's secular policies. The Islamic Revolution brought about sweeping changes in Iran's social, political, and economic landscape.

In such a context, my grandfather was a merchant and an entrepreneur. He dealt in essential goods like cooking oil and rice, as well as luxury products such as wine and meat, distributing them throughout the country. His thriving enterprise created jobs and opportunities for both Iranians and international workers in Iran, instilling in his children the values of hard work, accountability, and the importance of entrepreneurship.

But then everything changed. The winds of revolution swept through our nation, followed by the devastating Iran-Iraq war. Overnight, my grandfather's once-booming business was thrown into chaos, with much of his inventory rotting away in customs offices.

Rather than giving in to hopelessness, my grandfather made a choice to fight back against the circumstances. He salvaged what he could and turned his focus toward those suffering the most, the people living in the war-torn southern borders of Iran.

"I will build again," he declared, his voice filled with resolve.
"This is not a failure; it's just a setback."

And true to his word, he did just that. Clearing whatever goods he could from customs, he set out to rebuild not just his business, but also the lives of those affected by the ravages of war.

Towards the end of his life, when he fell seriously ill and was confined to his home, he began writing a book reflecting on his life as a business builder. Soon after, he lost the ability to write with his hands. It was then, as a teenage girl, that I began my first real executive training—writing on his behalf.

We would sit for hours, and he would recount his journey, all the ups and downs, the risks, the heartbreaks, and the small victories. I would carefully write down his memories, page by page, and tuck them neatly into a binder. I didn't realize it then, but that was the moment my education in entrepreneurship truly began.

The lessons I learned from him were practical, unfiltered, and deeply human. I could see how his decisions rippled across lives. How integrity, timing, and courage could change everything. For me, it wasn't just a story to document; it was a lifestyle to live: building something meaningful out of nothing but sweat, grit, and heart.

By the time I turned sixteen, that legacy had already taken root. I started my first business as a teenager; Not out of luxury, but necessity. I wanted to finance my dream of becoming a race car driver. It wasn't exactly the most conventional ambition for a young Iranian girl, but I was determined to do it on my own terms. I built small ventures, took on creative projects, and learned to manage risk before I could even legally drive on public roads.

Every Rial I earned went into funding track practices, tuning, equipment, and travel. Eventually, I became a professional test driver, and later, one of the few Iranian women to compete in racing events abroad.

That same combination of intuition and discipline, the ability to stay calm under pressure, to trust yourself at full speed, to know when to brake and when to accelerate, became the foundation of my entrepreneurial mindset. Racing taught me what my grandfather had embodied decades earlier: resilience isn't about never losing; it's about how fast you recover and rebuild.

Looking back, my journey has been shaped by that family DNA of reinvention. My grandfather rebuilt after the war. My parents built across industries and causes, factories, libraries, youth centers. And I've built across countries and systems, creating companies that merge design, innovation, and social impact.

If there's a through-line in all of it, it's that business, for me, is about purpose. Contrary to common practice and perception, business isn't about taking; it's fundamentally about giving.

Beyond mere profits, It's about designing systems that make life work better for others. And like my grandfather once said, when everything falls apart, you don't stop; you build again.

In the face of famine, war and decades of sanctions and uncertainty, my family became a living example of what entrepreneurship truly means. Through generations, they built, lost, and rebuilt again. Each time with more resilience, more creativity, and more faith in their ability to adapt. When the Iranian economy collapsed under sanctions, when inflation swallowed savings overnight, when opportunities seemed to vanish into thin air, they didn't wait for rescue. They created their own.

For my family, turning scarcity into possibility, finding dignity in self-reliance, and building systems of support when none existed was always survival turned into art. Every business decision was personal; every venture carried the weight of hope.

And even today, as Iran continues to navigate deep economic instability and isolation, that same spirit endures. My family, and countless others like them, keep pushing forward, not because the circumstances are easy, but because stopping isn't an option.

Their legacy lives not only in the stories we tell, but in the mindset they passed on to us: that to be an entrepreneur is to build even when the world is breaking; to design possibility out of impossibility.

All said above, what exactly is entrepreneurship by definition? It's a fair question. There are various types of entrepreneurship, each with its unique characteristics and focus.

And now, with the emergence of new technologies such as AI, Blockchain, and Self-Driving Cars, entrepreneurship's landscape is changing faster than ever. Let's take a look at different types of entrepreneurship.

Different Types of Entrepreneurship

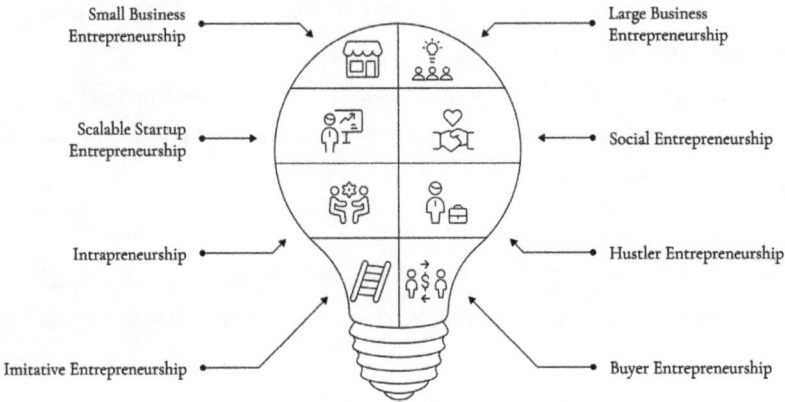

Small Business Entrepreneurship

Scalable Startup Entrepreneurship

Intrapreneurship

Imitative Entrepreneurship

Large Business Entrepreneurship

Social Entrepreneurship

Hustler Entrepreneurship

Buyer Entrepreneurship

As I learned, living among five generations of serial entrepreneurs and witnessing their work, entrepreneurship is a broad and dynamic concept that encompasses a variety of business models and strategies. It involves the creation, development, and management of a new venture to achieve an impact and generate profit to sustain the business. This can include starting a new business from scratch or reinvigorating an existing business through innovation, creativity, and strategic planning.

Entrepreneurs are individuals who take calculated risks (or sometimes, just jump head first into risks), identify opportunities, and leverage their skills and resources to create value and make a positive impact on society and the environment.

For them, entrepreneurship is more than just a career; it is a lifestyle choice that embodies freedom, creativity, and resilience. Entrepreneurs go on a journey that involves facing fears, overcoming challenges, and creating something unique. This lifestyle offers individuals the opportunity to be their own boss, make potentially unlimited income, choose their work hours, and pursue their passions, but there's no guarantee.

The path of an entrepreneur is characterized by constant growth. While the journey is filled with highs and lows, the rewards of building a successful business through hard work and determination are unparalleled. Ultimately, entrepreneurship is a way of life that requires courage, adaptability, and a relentless drive to create and succeed.

There is no single formula for being an entrepreneur. The essence of entrepreneurship is innovation and disruption, which defies being categorized or put into boxes. However, there are patterns when it comes to people who have built successful ventures several times, and we should try to learn from them.

Here are some recognized entrepreneurship patterns throughout the history:

1. Small Business Entrepreneurship

This is the most common type of entrepreneurship. It involves starting a business that typically has a small number of employees and is focused on serving a local market. This type includes local brick-and-mortar shops and services to a local region.[4]

My grandmother was a small business entrepreneur. She owned a local hairdressing shop frequented by celebrities. What I learned from her business was the importance of niching down. She excelled at her job, known for her signature style, and her services met the demanding standards of celebrities.

2. Large Business Entrepreneurship

Large business entrepreneurship refers to the entrepreneurial activities within established large companies. It involves innovating new products, services, and ideas based on market considerations, and fostering entrepreneurial behavior within the company to promote development, accommodate change, and generate value. Large business entrepreneurship is typically led by experienced business people with access to capital and resources that make it possible to grow.[5]

Examples of large business entrepreneurship include companies like Google, Disney, and Samsung, which innovate and reinvent their products and services to stay competitive. Large business entrepreneurship is distinct from small business entrepreneurship in that it is characterized by the presence of established operational capabilities, industry clout, and the ability to compete fiercely and influence the commercial environment. This type of entrepreneurship is suited for advanced professionals who know how to sustain innovation and growth within a large company's framework.

When I speak with early-stage founders who are nurturing an idea and endeavoring to launch their first venture, this is often the mindset they embrace: the aspiration to become the next Bill Gates, Oprah Winfrey, Richard Branson, Jeff Bezos, or Mark Zuckerberg. They envision themselves achieving monumental success, defying so many odds, and rising to the very top of their industry.

While this ambition is commendable—and certainly feasible in our world entrenched in late-stage capitalism, I must admit, I find it somewhat disheartening. Pursuing lofty ambitions and striving for excellence doesn't mandate that we all must seek to replicate the success of specific individuals.

My "Skeptical Optimism" approach to large business entrepreneurship offers me solace by not defining success solely based on the achievements of those with household names. Instead, it emphasizes the significance of being helpful, meaningful, and impactful in my own unique way.

For every big business entrepreneur, there are hundreds of other big business entrepreneurs - just not as big - that are doing great, making millions, and we don't know their names. I'm going to name some very important names, and you tell me how many of them you know by heart? How many of these very big entrepreneurs, who are Billionaires (Yes, with a B!), do you know?

Drew Houston[1], Cheng Wei[2], Alexander Karp[3], Orion Hindawi[4], Daniel Abraham[5], Wang Xing[6], Jin Sook and Do Won Chang[7], Jan Koum[8], Philip Anschutz[9].

---

1   American internet entrepreneur, CEO of Dropbox
2   Chinese billionaire, founder, chairman and CEO of DiDi
3   American entrepreneur, co-founder and CEO of Palantir Technologies
4   American software entrepreneur, co-founder of Tanium
5   American entrepreneur, known for creating the diet brand Slim-Fast
6   Chinese businessman, co-founder and CEO of Meituan
7   Married couple, Korean-American entrepreneurs who co-founded the retail chain Forever 21
8   Ukrainian-born American entrepreneur, co-founder of WhatsApp
9   American businessman, founder of The Anschutz Corporation

How many of these billionaires do you know? You may know some of their businesses, or you may not even know that. Each of them employs at least 1000 people, and is living quiet lives, unbothered by the so-called paparazzi!

3. Scalable Startup Entrepreneurship

Scalable startup entrepreneurship refers to the process of creating and growing a startup that has the potential to scale and become a large, successful business. This approach is often associated with the Lean Startup methodology, which emphasizes rapid experimentation, customer feedback, and iterative development to create a scalable and sustainable business model.[6]

Scalable startup entrepreneurship involves creating and growing a business that can adapt to changing market conditions, learn from customer feedback, and leverage technology to achieve long-term success.

Scalable model entrepreneurs are in my opinion, the smartest in the current economy. Let me explain why.

How a business works is by expanding. Expansion requires more money, more employees, more space, and more of everything. This runs the overhead to the roof and slashes the profits.

Now imagine having a business that as it grows, the expenses of it stays the same. This is scalable startup entrepreneurship. It is the art of finding ways, usually through technology that keep the cost down and eliminate the barriers of geography.

Almost every successful app on your phone is, or once was a scalable startup. Uber, Tinder, DuoLingo, Calm, Canva.

You build something that is replicable with the minimum amount of cost or provide a platform that connects people, and voila, you have yourself a scalable startup model. Some of the entrepreneurs in this category are more famous than large business entrepreneurs. Some of them you never learn their names.

Let me give you a firsthand example: As a Systemic Designer, I structured and founded **ENFA** (Euro Nordic Funding Alliance) to assist business owners and entrepreneurs from all walks of life in accessing cross-border business development and financing in a more streamlined and equitable manner.

The transacted capital is not mine, nor are the businesses. Since neither the capital nor the businesses depend on me or my team, it's a scalable model. Apart from infrastructural and community-building activities, it doesn't cost much more.

However, this doesn't imply that my team and I don't dedicate hours each day to developing the business and its surrounding community. We absolutely do! But it's scalable because there's a system in place that works for us.

4. Social Entrepreneurship

Social entrepreneurship refers to the practice of using entrepreneurial principles to create and manage businesses that address social or environmental problems. Social entrepreneurs aim to create sustainable solutions to social issues, often by leveraging innovative business models and technologies to achieve their goals.[7]

I know this type of entrepreneurship by heart. My mother is a social entrepreneur who dedicates her life to advocating "Freedom In Education" through her institutions and research. She believes that creativity should be facilitated and nurtured, not stifled by rigid structures. In her pursuit, she has pioneered innovative teaching methods that actively use the deep influence of story telling and encourage critical thinking, exploration of passion, and embracement of individuality. She firmly believes that every individual deserves the opportunity to learn in a manner that celebrates their unique strengths and interests - a fundamental inspiration behind this book.

From Iran's first specialized youth library, which attracted hundreds of youths, including myself, after school, to entrepreneurship and financial independence training for women in remote and poor areas of Iran, she has influenced the quality of life for thousands of families in Iran. In the documentary about her, "After The End," she references the obstacles in her journey and her tactics to overcome them.

This is the most powerful form of entrepreneurship, which affects the fabric of society, democratizes access to knowledge, and has ripple effects for generations to come — my inspiration for writing this book. Social entrepreneurs come in many forms and flavors. Some work with charities, some work with oppressed groups, and some focus on the daily lives of ordinary people. These entrepreneurs see what is going on, have a vision of a better future, and go on a quest to make that into reality.

5. Intrapreneurship

Intrapreneurs are individuals who act like entrepreneurs within their organizations taking risks, developing innovative ideas, and creating new products, services, or processes that drive growth. Intrapreneurship can take many forms: new business ventures, product or service innovation, process redesign, self-renewal, and even challenging the status quo when everyone else prefers stability. It thrives in environments that support experimentation, creativity, and autonomy, ensuring long-term sustainability and progress.[8]

After finishing my studies, I had to secure a full-time job to stay in Norway as an immigrant from Iran. I was hired as a Service and Systemic Designer at one of the country's largest financial institutions, DNB bank—the first employee in my family's history. I was terrified. I didn't know how to navigate this new life. I constantly feared making mistakes and not meeting expectations. I was used to understanding things my own way, finding creative solutions freely. Suddenly, I was in a world of strict hours, predefined templates, and fixed processes. For the first few months, I felt completely lost.

On the bright side, I was among the first designers hired there, which meant no one really knew what my job should look like. That uncertainty became my opportunity.

I defined my own role, created systems from scratch, and helped shape an environment where design could actually thrive. Over time, our small, curious group of designers grew into a tight-knit community of innovators, each of us playing the role of an intrapreneur in our own way.

By the time I left five years later to focus on my own ventures, the innovation department had grown into a major force within the company. It was proof that when people are given freedom, trust, and a bit of room to experiment, they can transform even the most traditional structures from within.

Being an intrapreneur is one of the most underrated roles in the modern business world. Yet, I believe it's exactly what today's organizations have to embrace most. Time and again, we see once-dominant companies lose their edge, not because they lack resources or talent, but because they fear vision. They hesitate to empower the people who think differently, and when they do bring them in, they confine them to boxes, smothering the very spark that could have reignited their relevance.

How many brands as such can you name?

Nokia is very bold in my mind. My first cellphone was a Nokia phone. It was THE BRAND to have. It used to be disruptive, edgy, and new. But Nokia grew and didn't innovate enough. So it became a phone for older people, until a point when no one knew it was a phone brand at all.

I had a conversation with my cousin - a Gen Alpha - recently, who had no idea what a Nokia was. Yes, the brand still exists and is profitable.

But Nokia has transitioned from its iconic phone-making business to focusing on network equipment and licensing. The company remains active in the telecoms industry, specializing in telecom networks. It has undergone significant changes, including selling its phone business, experiencing layoffs, and refocusing its operations on network equipment.[9]

What Nokia could have in the early 2010s was an intrapreneur. Someone who had the guts to do some market research, see the trends early on, and challenge the management to let go of their designs and technology while they were still making billions from it. Had that happened, you would have probably had a phone with a renewed Symbian OS, and the stocks of Apple were not priced at nearly $200 a share. Intrapreneurship is not what the world wants (at least the world of successful big entrepreneurs), but what the world needs.

6. Hustler Entrepreneurship

People who are willing to work hard and put in constant effort are considered hustler entrepreneurs. As is often the case, they start small and work towards growing a bigger business with hard work rather than capital. In entrepreneurship, hustling means doing whatever it takes, legally, for your startup to be successful.

While this is not a scientific term, it's widely accepted in entrepreneurship circles and has a culture revolving around it, commonly known as the hustle culture.

If you've seen the plaques that say "Hustle Harder" on them anywhere, in a coworking space, an accelerator, or on your Instagram feed, consider yourself introduced to the Hustle Culture.

As of now, it mainly consists of people who have a 9-5 job that they wish to quit or have just quit. I like to call these Hustlers, the transition entrepreneurs.

As you have come to understand, entrepreneurship is not something you can dip in and out of and get results. It's a lifestyle. So hustlers either become full-time entrepreneurs or go back to being an employee. A hustle very rarely stays a hustle. A successful hustle turns into a full-blown business, and a failed one fades away.

I would hate to discredit this culture, as it is the gateway to freedom for so many. The so-called Mommy-Entrepreneurs (not a term I'd like to use), are a big part of this movement. They build something from their home while taking care of their babies, and as their child grows, so does their business.

Natalie Ellis (Boss Babe), a big hustler, now a successful entrepreneur with a net worth of over 20 Million Dollars, was once a mom who posted her personal health journey on Instagram and how she wanted to be an entrepreneur. She now teaches other women like her to become entrepreneurs. She has a community that helps women founders with educational resources and networking events, and still is, a so-called stay-at-home mom.[10]

7. Imitative Entrepreneurship

Imitative entrepreneurship refers to the process of creating a business by copying or adapting an existing concept or business model. In contrast to innovative entrepreneurs who invent new ideas, products, or production methods, Imitative entrepreneurs replicate an existing business idea, product, or service with slight modifications in a different market or location. They rely on market validation and existing demand, and while they may not be as innovative as other entrepreneur types, they work towards improving existing business ideas.[11]

Imitative entrepreneurship is characterized by the adoption and imitation of profitable business concepts, tactics, or goods that have previously proven to be viable and marketable. While imitation is a characteristic, entrepreneurs should strive for responsible competition, ensuring they add value and differentiate themselves within the market they enter.

Examples of imitative entrepreneurs include the Samwer brothers, known for cloning companies such as eBay, Airbnb, Facebook, Pinterest, and Groupon in Europe.

China is also a big destination for Imitative Entrepreneurs. In the hit TV series "Silicon Valley", the character named Jian Yang, spent time with the innovators and startups in the States, only to go back to China and copy all of them. While this was a comedy depiction of what imitative entrepreneurship looks like, it's not far from the truth when it comes to countries that experience economic sanctions. Russia, China, Iran. Give it a try and Google and find the exact replicas of Netflix, Uber, or any other app for that matter. You will find them easily. Some even have features far more developed than their originals.

However, it would be an understatement and a cruelty to reduce this type of entrepreneurship to just copy and paste. Sometimes, it is much more complex, because the entrepreneur has to analyze the cultural, social, and economic intricacies of the place they want to run their business in. Sometimes, they start with copying a business model, and they improve upon that which is admirable and necessary.

In most cases, the copies are run far better in terms of financial health of the business, and management of resources, including employees. Copies help the originals to always stay on edge and be competitive.

Without imitation, we only would see one business monopolizing an industry, and when a business consolidates so much power, corruption happens.

I have personal experience of using Snapp!, which is an Iranian imitation of Uber. It has features that are custom-made for an Islamic country, such as having a woman driver to pick up women, - only if you want to - and allows users to share their live location with the police and a family member.[12]

I had a long debate with myself, about using services that are copied in Iran, but then I came to an illuminating conclusion for myself.

I thought, what would happen to the thousands of people whose livelihood depends on Snapp! If this service were to shut down. How would ordinary people get from A to B in Iran? Is it the fault of the people, the ordinary Sams and Susans (by the way, both Iranian names!), that their country is under sanction and their government is not a signatory of the copyright law? Are they to suffer and live a backward life, or is it the duty of the innovators of this country to bring the same level of comfort to their citizens regardless? - called survival?

I let you draw your own conclusion, as imitative entrepreneurship sometimes has some grey areas. It's all up for interpretation.

8. Buyer Entrepreneurship

Buyer entrepreneurship is a type of entrepreneurship where an individual purchases an existing company or business and actively works to grow and expand it. Unlike investors, a buyer entrepreneur is involved both financially and personally in the business, remaining active and directly helping the investment to grow.[13]

Examples of buyer entrepreneurs include individuals who purchase existing businesses, such as Google, which has bought many smaller businesses, or sole proprietors who want to expand their portfolio, like property investors.

This type of entrepreneurship has been around for the longest time, with partners buying each other out of the business, or a whole new party coming out and acquiring a business. It's one of the most viable exit strategies for many scalable startup entrepreneurs who want to make money and move on to their next adventure.

While I have my personal preferences in entrepreneurship and have first-hand experience in some, I need to reiterate just as I did at the beginning of this point, that entrepreneurship, by nature, is ever-changing and people have their own unique viewpoints on it. I am here to tell you that all is fair.

However, I feel the need to discuss the difference between building a startup (what most people mean by entrepreneurship these days), owning a business, and being an entrepreneur. This question was at the top of my FAQ list if I ever were to build one!

Granted, the lines between them may be blury, but there are distinctions nonetheless which I believe are more important than most people realize. I simply think that most idea or IP holders who join an incubator or accelerator are under the wrong impression that their impact could only be generated within the framework of what they will be taught in those programs, while there are also many other ways besides building a startup to drive the value they are after.

Entrepreneurship vs Owning a Business vs Building a Startup

Having worked across continents, from the structured systems of Northern Europe to the entrepreneurial improvisation of Africa and the fast-paced innovation hubs of North America and Asia, I've seen how differently people interpret entrepreneurship. Some treat it as founding a startup, others see it as running a family business, and a few understand it as a mindset that transcends ownership entirely. All of them are valid, but they are not the same.

In Silicon Valley, for instance, "entrepreneurship" has become almost synonymous with "startups." The culture there revolves around disruption, speed, and scalability, the race to become the next unicorn. A founder with an idea can raise millions based on a pitch deck, and the measure of success is often how fast the company grows rather than how deeply it impacts people. It's a system that has produced remarkable breakthroughs, think of Stripe or Airbnb, but also one that has normalized unsustainable pressure and short-term thinking.

Meanwhile, in many parts of Europe, particularly in Germany or Italy, entrepreneurship is more deeply rooted in craftsmanship and legacy. The "Mittelstand" — small to mid-sized, often family-run companies — are not startups chasing valuations; they are long-term businesses obsessed with quality, precision, and incremental improvement. These companies may not make headlines, but they build economies. Their innovation is quiet, steady, and profoundly human.[14]

And then, in emerging economies like Kenya or India, entrepreneurship often looks entirely different again, it's a necessity, not a choice. People innovate not because they have venture funding, but because they must. A street vendor who builds a micro-distribution network for solar lamps or a young coder in Lagos creating a fintech solution to bypass unreliable banking systems — these are entrepreneurs in the truest sense. They may never use the word "startup," but they embody innovation, resilience, and social impact.

So yes, the distinctions between owning a business, starting a startup, and being an entrepreneur are real and meaningful. A startup is a temporary structure built to find a scalable, repeatable business model. A business is a stable vehicle that delivers consistent value over time. And entrepreneurship is the underlying mindset, the ability to see opportunity, take risks, and create value where others see barriers.

The problem today is that we've allowed the startup narrative to dominate the entire conversation. Incubators and accelerators, while invaluable, often teach founders to chase scale before substance, to think that their worth lies in the funding rounds they raise rather than the systems they build or the problems they solve. I've seen so many brilliant founders get trapped in that cycle:

refining pitch decks instead of their products, optimizing metrics instead of their missions.

Entrepreneurship, in its truest form, doesn't always need to look like a Silicon Valley story. It might look like a small-town factory that has reinvented itself over generations, or a local café that turned sustainability into a lifestyle brand. The key is to understand what kind of builder you are — whether you're innovating within an existing business, creating a scalable model from scratch, or crafting stability through ownership. When you know that, when you stop confusing the frameworks and start embracing your path, you stop chasing borrowed definitions of success. You begin to build your own, and that is where Design can help.

Design as a Principle of Change

When I was 18, my mother — a renowned social entrepreneur — decided it was time for me to learn something no classroom could teach. She arranged for me to visit some of the less privileged parts of Iran, so I could understand life beyond the comfort I had always known. My destination was a small town near Kerman, devastated years earlier by the Bam earthquake.

She had organized for me to teach physics to a group of teenage girls living in an orphanage, children who had lost their parents in the disaster. My class consisted of two dozen girls, most of them not much younger than me. I arrived full of enthusiasm, convinced I'd be teaching them about Newton's laws and the elegance of scientific equations. I imagined writing formulas on the blackboard while they listened attentively and took notes. I couldn't have been more wrong.

From the very first day, I realized that my world and theirs were miles apart. While I was eager to talk about gravity and energy, they were giggling about weddings, describing what their dream ceremonies would look like, down to the color of the ribbons and dresses. To them, marriage wasn't just romance; it was escape. Freedom from poverty, from uncertainty, from a life that felt too heavy for girls their age.

They weren't concerned about university or careers — at least, not in the way I was. And who could blame them? They saw me as someone from another planet: privileged, educated, and protected, all of which was, in their eyes, far from their reality. Their world was one of survival, not ambition. These girls had lost homes, parents, siblings, and yet they called themselves lucky. They had survived what so many hadn't.

Over time, I realized something deep. It wasn't that they lacked curiosity or intelligence, it was that they had lost the ability to dream. The earthquake had taken more than their families and homes; it had taken their confidence to risk failure, to imagine something more.

Their mindset had become one of preservation: if I don't try, I can't fail. There's a Persian saying that captures it perfectly:

"The essay you haven't written has no mistakes."

"دیکته نانوشته غلط ندارد"

That realization hit me hard. I couldn't reach them through formulas and theories, I had to meet them where they were. So, I changed my approach. The next day, instead of staying in the classroom, I took them outside. We sat under the shade of trees, and I told them the story of Newton and the falling apple. They listened — really listened — for the first time. The following week, I told them about Archimedes and his "Eureka" moment. We gathered around a small pool, dropping objects into the water and watching what floated and what sank. Laughter filled the air. What had once been a dull physics class became an exploration, playful, alive, and curious.

We even ventured into the theory of relativity, asking wild questions like: "Does the water's weight slightly change Earth's gravity?" or "How much lighter do we become underwater?" The science wasn't perfect, but the wonder was. They were thinking, questioning, experimenting — and most importantly, dreaming.

I learned then that sometimes the best classroom has no walls. Under the open sky, surrounded by laughter, curiosity, and the occasional goat wandering by, those girls began to see science not as something distant, but as something they could touch.

Slowly, their conversations began to change, from weddings to universities, from escape to ambition. I could see a spark returning. It wasn't me changing them; it was the environment. Simply shifting the space they learned in changed the way they thought.

Years later, I realized how fundamental that lesson was. The spaces we inhabit, physical, emotional, and mental, shape the way we think, act, and grow. That experience was my first real encounter with Design as a transformative force, long before I ever heard the term.

When I began to formally study design, I realized that what I had done back in Kerman was precisely what great designers do every day: observe, empathize, reframe the problem, and co-create solutions. I hadn't designed a product—I had redesigned an experience. I hadn't taught physics, I had designed curiosity.

That experience stayed with me and shaped how I approach every project, venture, and collaboration since. Because design, when done right, is human at its core.

Design is the invisible architecture of change. It's what turns challenges into opportunities, what transforms fear into curiosity, and what gives form to hope. It allows us to imagine futures that don't yet exist, and then build the systems to make them real.

So when people ask me what design really means, I tell them this: design is not what you make, it's what you enable.

And that lesson, born under the trees of a ruined city, surrounded by laughter and questions, became the foundation of how I see the world and the work I do today.

Chapter 2:
The Multiverse of Making

I was fortunate enough to be born in Isfahan, a city often called the Paris of Iran, where architecture doesn't just exist; it breathes. The city is a living museum of geometry, poetry, and light. I grew up walking down Chahar Bagh, a boulevard inspired by the Champs-Élysées, its tree-lined symmetry a lesson in balance and proportion. I spent countless afternoons crossing Isfahan's 400-year-old bridges, watching sunlight ripple across the Zayandeh River as if the city were in quiet conversation with time. When I needed to escape the noise of the world, I would lie on the cool tiles of the Sheikh Lotfollah Mosque, looking up at its radiant dome as beams of light filtered through like divine brushstrokes, a masterclass in how design can evoke emotion.

It was no surprise that I chose to study architecture. My father, an entrepreneur in heavy engineering and construction, had introduced me to the world of buildings from an early age. Through his travels, photos, and stories, I learned to look beyond facades and into the systems that hold them together, the unseen frameworks that make beauty functional and function beautiful. Working with him shaped my understanding of how design and industry intertwine, and how every structure carries a story about the people who inhabit it.

Years later, when I applied for a master's degree abroad and found myself being interviewed Architectural Association (AA) in London, I thought my path was set. The interview went remarkably well, so well, in fact, that the head of the school's program asked to meet me during his trip to Iran. We spent hours talking about architecture, culture, and the responsibility of creators in shaping the world. As our conversation drew to a close, he looked at me and said something that would quietly redirect the course of my life:

"Nilu, you have a place at our school if you want it.
But if I may be honest, I think you might be more of a designer than an architect."

His words caught me off guard. I asked him why. He told me that what stood out in my portfolio wasn't just the drawings or concepts, it was the way I thought. My fascination with human behavior, with systems, with the why behind things rather than just the what. Architecture, he said, demands an extraordinary kind of patience, sometimes decades pass before you see your vision realized. Design, however, allows for more immediacy, experimentation, and dialogue with the people you're creating for.

I didn't take his words as a dismissal of architecture. Quite the opposite, architecture remains, to me, one of the highest forms of human expression. It's the art of giving structure to civilization. But in that moment, I understood something about myself: I was drawn to a different rhythm. I wanted to work within living systems, to experiment, to iterate, and to witness the social impact of my work within a human lifetime.

When I later applied to the University of Oslo, I was accepted into their design program, but not for architecture. It felt like the universe gently nudging me toward a path I hadn't yet imagined for myself. So, I packed my bags and moved to Norway, stepping into a world where design was not just about buildings or objects, but about systems, services, and ideas.

Design was new to me, but it felt familiar, almost ancestral. The more I studied it, the more I realized that design is not a modern invention; it's a fundamental human instinct. It's how we have shaped our tools, our cities, and our cultures since the beginning of time. Architecture had given me an appreciation for permanence and vision. Design gave me the freedom to explore change, adaptability, and the beauty of impermanence.

And in that balance, between structure and fluidity, tradition and experimentation, I found my home.

History of Design
(Not interested? Fast forward to page 47)

The historical context of design in society is a rich blend that has significantly influenced human progress, commerce, and innovation. From ancient civilizations to the present day, design has played a pivotal role in shaping entrepreneurial activity and societal development.

In ancient civilizations such as Mesopotamia, Egypt, Greece, and Rome, design served both utilitarian and symbolic purposes. From architecture and pottery to jewelry and clothing, design differentiated commodities and reflected cultural values and beliefs[15].

In Mesopotamia, for example, intricate clay tablets and cylinder seals were not only practical tools but also works of art that communicated important information and demonstrated the craftsmanship of their creators. Similarly, the grand temples and palaces of ancient Egypt showcased the mastery of architects and artisans while serving as symbols of power and divine authority.

During the Middle Ages, design became closely intertwined with craftsmanship and trade through the establishment of guilds. These associations of artisans and merchants regulated the production and sale of goods, emphasizing the importance of quality, skill, and innovation. Craft guilds, such as the Worshipful Company of Goldsmiths in London, ensured standards of excellence in metalwork and jewelry design, fostering a culture of apprenticeship and mastery. The guild system not only preserved traditional techniques but also provided a platform for collaboration and exchange, fueling creativity and entrepreneurship.

In the modern era, design has emerged as a driving force behind entrepreneurship and innovation, permeating every aspect of business and commerce. From graphic design and branding to user experience and product development, design thinking has become essential for organizations seeking to create value and differentiate themselves in competitive markets. Designers such as Dieter Rams[1] and Jonathan Ive[2] have championed principles of simplicity, usability, and sustainability, influencing the design of everything from consumer electronics to furniture.

The rise of digital technologies has further expanded the scope of design, enabling new forms of expression and interaction in areas such as web design, app development, and virtual reality.

In the crucible of the 20th century, design transcended its traditional role as mere ornamentation and emerged as a potent strategic tool for businesses seeking to carve out their niches in the fiercely competitive marketplace. This epoch witnessed a profound shift in the perception of design, from an afterthought to a cornerstone of corporate strategy, from an embellishment to an essential element in the quest for differentiation and market dominance.

Central to this transformation was the burgeoning discipline of branding, which took root and flourished amidst the tumultuous landscape of consumer culture. Design, with its ability to evoke emotions, convey messages, and shape perceptions, became the linchpin of branding efforts, enabling companies to forge distinctive identities, establish emotional connections with consumers, and

---

1   Dieter Rams is a German industrial designer who is most closely associated with the consumer products company Braun, the furniture company Vitsœ, and the functionalist school of industrial design.

2   Sir Jonathan Paul Ive is a British-American designer. He is best known for his work at Apple Inc., where he was senior vice president of industrial design and chief design officer. Ive is the founder of LoveFrom, a creative collective that works with Ferrari, Airbnb, OpenAI and other global brands.

command premium prices for their products and services.

The realm of corporate identity design emerged as a pivotal battleground, where companies vied for attention, recognition, and loyalty in an increasingly crowded marketplace. Logos, color schemes, typography, and visual imagery became the building blocks of brand identities, imbuing them with personality, character, and meaning. From the iconic golden arches of McDonald's to the swoosh of Nike, from the interlocking rings of Audi to the bitten apple of Apple, these symbols transcended their material forms to become indelible markers of corporate identity and cultural significance.

Packaging design also assumed newfound importance as businesses recognized its power to influence purchasing decisions and shape brand perceptions at the point of sale. Packaging became more than just a container, it became a silent salesman, communicating brand values, product attributes, and promises of quality through its form, materials, and graphic design. The sleek contours of an iPhone box, the vibrant colors of a Coca-Cola can, the minimalist elegance of a Chanel perfume bottle, each of these artifacts of design spoke volumes about the brands they represented, inviting consumers into a world of aspiration, desire, and fulfillment.

Advertising, too, underwent a metamorphosis as design took center stage in the battle for consumers' hearts and minds. Print ads, billboards, television commercials, and later, digital media, became canvases for creative expression, where visual storytelling, imagery, and typography converged to captivate audiences, communicate brand messages, and drive sales. Whether it was Volkswagen's timeless "Think Small" campaign, Apple's groundbreaking "1984" commercial, or Coca-Cola's iconic "Hilltop" ad, these landmark campaigns demonstrated the power of design to transcend the confines of commerce and resonate with the collective consciousness of society.[16]

In this brave new world of design-driven business, the role of designers evolved from mere stylists to strategic thinkers, collaborators, and problem solvers. Design thinking, a human-centered approach to innovation that emphasizes empathy, experimentation, and iteration, became the modus operandi for companies seeking to navigate the complexities of the modern marketplace and create meaningful experiences for their customers.

As the 20th century drew to a close, the influence of design on business continued to grow, permeating every aspect of the corporate ecosystem, from product development to customer service, from employee engagement to sustainability initiatives. Design has become not just a strategic tool, but a cultural force, shaping the way we live, work, and interact with the world around us.

Thus, in the annals of business history, the 20th century stands as a testament to the transformative power of design, a power that transcends aesthetics to touch the very heart of human experience, shaping our perceptions, our preferences, and our aspirations in ways both profound and enduring.

As the 21st century dawned, the digital revolution ushered in a new era of unprecedented change and innovation, transforming the way we live, work, and interact with the world around us. At the heart of this seismic shift was the profound impact of technology on the practice of design, propelling it into new frontiers of creativity, collaboration, and user-centered innovation.

The advent of the digital age brought with it a host of challenges and opportunities for designers and entrepreneurs alike.

On one hand, the rapid pace of technological advancement and the proliferation of digital platforms presented daunting new complexities and uncertainties. On the other hand, they offered boundless new possibilities for creativity, connectivity, and disruption.

Central to this transformation was the evolution of design towards a relentless focus on user experience (UX) and interaction design (IxD), reflecting a fundamental shift in priorities from aesthetics to functionality, from form to usability. In the realm of digital products and services, where the interface between humans and machines has become increasingly seamless and ubiquitous, the user experience emerged as the linchpin of success, driving customer satisfaction, loyalty, and engagement.

Designers embraced a user-centered approach, leveraging insights from psychology, anthropology, and cognitive science to understand and empathize with the needs, preferences, and behaviors of their users. User research, personas, journey mapping, and usability testing became standard tools in the designer's toolkit, enabling them to create products and services that were intuitive, accessible, and delightful to use.

The rise of artificial intelligence (AI) and machine learning further expanded the horizons of design, unlocking new possibilities for personalization, automation, and predictive analytics. AI-powered algorithms analyze vast troves of data to anticipate user needs, tailor experiences in real-time, and drive decision-making across a myriad of industries, from e-commerce to healthcare, from finance to entertainment.

Moreover, AI itself became a powerful tool in the hands of designers, augmenting their creative capabilities, automating repetitive tasks, and enabling them to explore new frontiers of generative design, evolutionary algorithms, and computational creativity. From chatbots to recommendation engines, from image recognition to natural language processing, AI has become an integral part of the designer's toolkit, empowering them to create more intelligent, responsive, and adaptive experiences for users.

Meanwhile, the proliferation of digital platforms and the democratization of design tools fueled a renaissance of creativity and entrepreneurship, opening doors for aspiring designers and startups to bring their visions to life and disrupt established industries.

Crowdfunding platforms like Kickstarter and Indiegogo provided a launchpad for innovative products and services, while online marketplaces like Etsy and Shopify offered a global stage for independent designers and makers to showcase and sell their creations.

The boundaries between design disciplines blurred as designers embraced multidisciplinary collaboration and hybrid skill sets, transcending traditional silos to tackle complex, multifaceted challenges.

Designers became not just creators of artifacts, but orchestrators of experiences, systems thinkers, and agents of change, shaping the future of business, technology, and society.

As the 21st century unfolds, the journey of design continues to evolve, driven by the inexorable march of technology, the shifting sands of culture, and the imperatives of human experience. Yet amidst the whirlwind of change, one thing remains constant—the enduring power of design to inspire, innovate, and elevate the human spirit, illuminating the path forward in an ever-changing world.

Now you know that design is nothing new. Granted, it has been the new buzzword of the decade, and every field of work and study has added design to its principles of practice, but at its core, design is simple, ancient, and most importantly, crucial and effective.

Design is so intertwined in every aspect of our lives that sometimes just for fun, I challenge people to come up with a field of work that has no need for it. From arts to education, entrepreneurship to HR, I can't find a single field where design is irrelevant.

I have a friend who is a medical doctor, and she once told me that except for plastic surgery, there's no other need for design in their field. It was a long heated conversation, in which I pointed out that every stitch a doctor makes is with design, every tool they use in the operation room is a product of design to work best in that environment, and every procedure they had to follow in patient care was also a product of human-centric design, ensuring the possible experience for the patient.

So believe me when I say passionately that design is everywhere.

EVERYWHERE.

No history review is complete without a deep dive into its schools of thought. So bear with me as I take you through the journey of design.

Design's Schools of Thought

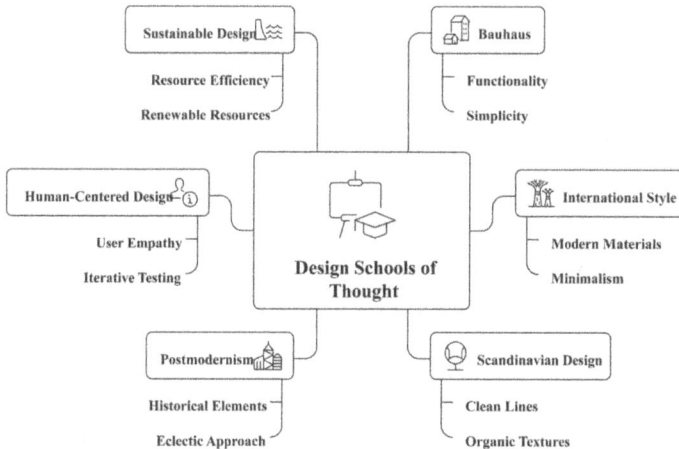

Design encompasses a broad spectrum of disciplines, each influenced by distinct schools of thought that have evolved over time. These schools of thought provide philosophical, methodological, and practical frameworks through which designers approach problems, create solutions, and influence aesthetics. Let's delve into a few notable design schools of thought:

1. Bauhaus (1919-1933)

Originating in Germany, the Bauhaus school of thought emphasized the unity of art, craft, and technology. It sought to bring together all forms of creative expression into a single, functional design that was accessible to the masses. Bauhaus's teachings prioritized functionality and simplicity, with a focus on geometric forms, rationality, and the absence of superfluous decoration. The legacy of the Bauhaus is profound, influencing architecture, furniture design, graphic design, and industrial design, promoting the idea that good design should be part of everyday life.[17]

2. International Style (1920s-1960s)

The International Style is a major architectural style that emerged in the 1920s and 1930s. It was characterized by an emphasis on volume over mass, the use of

45

lightweight, mass-produced materials, and the rejection of ornamental details. This school of thought favored functionality, simplicity, and the use of modern materials like steel, glass, and concrete to create sleek, minimalist structures. The International Style played a crucial role in the development of modernist architecture around the world.[18]

3. Scandinavian Design (1950s-present)

The scandinavian design emphasizes simplicity, minimalism, and functionality, drawing on the conditions and values of life in Nordic countries. This design philosophy is known for its clean lines, organic textures, and a strong connection to natural elements. It also emphasizes democratic design, with the idea that good design should be accessible to all. Scandinavian design has had a lasting impact on interior design, furniture, and product design, promoting the idea that beauty and functionality can coexist harmoniously.[19]

4. Postmodernism (1970s-present)

Emerging as a reaction against austerity, formality, and lack of variety in modern design, postmodernism embraces complexity and contradiction.

This school of thought is characterized by the revival of historical elements, the mixing of different styles and mediums, and a playful, eclectic approach. Postmodernism challenges the modernist principles of simplicity and functionality, advocating for designs that are expressive, dynamic, and imbued with meaning.[20]

5. Human-Centered Design (1980s-present)

Human-centered design (HCD) is a problem-solving approach that focuses on understanding the needs, wants, and limitations of end-users at the outset of the design process. This school of thought prioritizes empathy for users, advocating for the design of products, services, and systems that are tailored to their experiences and needs. HCD involves iterative testing, a multidisciplinary approach, and a commitment to creating solutions that improve human well-being and user satisfaction.[21]

6. Sustainable Design (1990s-present)

Sustainable design prioritizes environmental considerations and the well-being of future generations. This approach seeks to minimize the negative impacts of design on the environment through the efficient use of resources, reduction of pollution and waste, and the promotion of renewable resources. Sustainable design spans various disciplines, including architecture, product design, and urban planning, emphasizing the importance of creating eco-friendly and sustainable solutions in response to climate change and environmental degradation.[22]

Each of these schools of thought has contributed to the evolution of design as a discipline, reflecting changes in technology, culture, and societal values. They offer diverse perspectives on how design can solve problems, enhance human experiences, and shape our built environment. As the field of design continues to evolve, it's likely that new schools of thought will emerge, responding to future challenges and opportunities.

Design as a Multiverse of Disciplines

As you see, design has expanded its territory significantly over time, infiltrating various fields and domains beyond its traditional boundaries. This expansion has been driven by a combination of technological advancements, societal changes, and evolving attitudes towards the role of design in addressing complex challenges.

In another word, if entrepreneurship is about building, then design is about imagining what's worth building in the first place. It's the discipline that turns ideas into experiences, visions into systems, and challenges into opportunities. Design gives form to intention. It's how meaning takes shape, whether in a product, a service, a policy, or even a way of thinking.

And yet, design is not one thing. It's a multiverse, it's a living, breathing multiverse. Once limited to art studios and architectural drawings, design today extends into every corner of human life. It shapes not only what we see and touch, but also how we think, behave, organize, and imagine the future. This evolution didn't happen overnight.

It emerged from humanity's growing complexity, our technological leaps, social struggles, and ecological realities. As our world intertwined across systems, so did design. It evolved from a discipline that makes things beautiful into one that makes things possible.

At its highest level sits **Systemic Design**, which zooms out to view entire ecosystems—social, economic, environmental—and reimagines how they connect. It's used to tackle challenges like urban poverty, food systems, or public health, helping us see relationships rather than isolated problems.

Service Design builds on that idea but moves closer to everyday life. It choreographs how we experience systems, how a patient moves through a hospital, how a citizen interacts with government services, or how a traveler checks into an airline. It considers what we see ("front stage") and what we don't ("backstage"), ensuring that even the most complex systems feel effortless and human.

In our digital age, **UI (User Interface)** and **UX (User Experience)** Design have become the visual and emotional languages of technology. They dictate how we touch, swipe, and feel our way through digital worlds, whether we're ordering food, learning online, or connecting with loved ones halfway across the globe.

Meanwhile, **Graphic Design** and **Visual Communication** remain timeless, shaping how ideas are seen and understood. A symbol, a poster, a campaign, these are the cultural vessels through which societies express values and identities.

Industrial Design reminds us that the physical world is still central. Every chair, car, lamp, and device we use carries the invisible imprint of design thinking, balancing ergonomics, sustainability, and aesthetics in one harmonious form.

Interaction Design and Experience **Design (XD)** bring choreography to life, whether physical, digital, or emotional. They remind us that great design isn't just what we see; it's how we move, feel, and remember.

And then there's **Environmental and Interior Design**, which considers not only the beauty of a space but also its psychology. It shapes how we live, learn, and collaborate, whether in a family home, an open office, or an entire city.

Fashion Design turns identity into form. Beyond trends, fashion tells stories of culture, resistance, and belonging. In recent years, fashion has also become a testing ground for **Circular Design**, where clothes are created, reused, and reborn rather than discarded.

Motion Design, **Game Design**, and **Sound Design** expand the sensory frontier, merging creativity with immersion. They engage not only sight but also rhythm, emotion, and interactivity, reminding us that design can be felt as much as it can be seen.

Then comes **Sustainable and Regenerative Design**, where designers think like nature, creating systems that give back more than they take. It's the difference between designing a product and designing an ecosystem.

Data Visualization and **Predictive Design** use creativity to make sense of information. One translates numbers into stories; the other uses AI and behavioral insight to anticipate what humans might need next—often before they know it themselves.

Universal Design challenges the notion of "average." It asks: how can we design products, spaces, and systems that work for everyone, regardless of age, ability, or circumstance? It's not just accessibility; it's empathy turned into structure.

Then there's **Design Anthropology**, a bridge between culture and creativity. It studies how people live, interact, and adapt, and uses those insights to shape more meaningful products and systems. It's design rooted in humanity, not in assumptions.

Behavioral Design dives into psychology, exploring how environments and systems can gently nudge people toward better decisions, saving energy, making healthier choices, or collaborating more effectively.

In the world of organizations, **Organizational Design** and **Policy Design** are redefining leadership. They apply design thinking to internal structures and governance, crafting workplaces and policies that are human-centered, adaptable, and resilient.

And at the edges of imagination lies **Speculative Design** and **Futures Design**, disciplines that ask "what if?" They explore possible futures, from sustainable cities to post-capitalist economies, not to predict them but to design pathways toward them.

Together, these fields form a vast constellation. Each discipline has its own tools and languages, but they all share one core belief: that design is about shaping relationships, between people, between systems, between the present and what's possible.

Design today is not just about things. It's about connections. It's how we move from what is to what could be.

Exercise: Mapping Your Design Universe

You don't need to be a designer to think like one. Every entrepreneur, policymaker, or changemaker touches design in some way—often without realizing it. This exercise is about uncovering your personal "design universe."

Step 1: Trace Your Interactions
Think about your last 24 hours. Which designs did you interact with—physical, digital, or invisible? Maybe it was the layout of your workspace, the onboarding process of an app, or the flow of your morning commute. Write down five that stood out (good or bad).

Step 2: Identify the Discipline Behind Them
Next to each example, note the type of design that shaped it—UX, service, policy, interior, behavioral, etc. You'll begin to see how diverse design truly is.

Step 3: Map the Connections
On a blank page, draw circles for each type of design you interact with most often. Connect them with lines where they overlap—like when digital design meets service design, or when sustainability meets fashion.

Step 4: Reflect on Your Role
Ask yourself: which of these designs do I influence in my work or life? Where could I apply design principles—empathy, prototyping, systems thinking—to make something better?

Step 5: Imagine Your Future Design Role
If you were to expand your "design universe," which new discipline would you explore? How might that shift your approach to problem-solving, leadership, or innovation?

Remember: design isn't a profession. It's a way of seeing. And the more lenses you collect, the clearer the world—and its possibilities—become.

Designer's Approach to the World

Designers see the world differently. Where others see obstacles, they see opportunities. Where some accept what is, designers ask what could be. This perspective is not limited to those trained in design; it is a way of thinking, a mindset that anyone can adopt to navigate life's complexities and reimagine its possibilities.

At the heart of a designer's approach lies curiosity. Designers are perpetual learners, observing the world with an open mind and questioning the status quo. They study patterns, uncover hidden connections, and search for unmet needs, not out of obligation, but out of a genuine desire to improve what exists.

Empathy is their compass. Designers don't create for themselves; they create for others. They step into the shoes of users, stakeholders, and communities, seeking to understand their experiences, challenges, and aspirations. It's this deep understanding that makes their solutions not only functional but meaningful.

Iteration is their engine. Designers know that the first attempt is rarely the best. They embrace failure as part of the process, using it to refine their ideas and push boundaries. Each prototype, sketch, or draft is a conversation between what works and what doesn't, leading to solutions that are tested, thoughtful, and ready to make an impact.

Above all, designers are dreamers grounded in practicality. They imagine bold futures and then work step by step to bring them to life. They thrive in ambiguity, balancing creativity with structure, and ideas with execution. For a designer, no problem is too complex, no vision too ambitious, only challenges waiting to be tackled with intention and care.

To approach the world as a designer is to embrace the unknown, to believe in progress, and to act with purpose. It's about seeing every roadblock as a design challenge, every interaction as an opportunity, and every morning as a fresh chance to create something better.

Chapter 3:
Building by Design:
The New Age of Entrepreneurs

I launched my second venture, an interior architecture firm, during my bachelor's studies in Iran. It was inspired by my experience in Kerman, where I had witnessed how space and experience can shape human behavior, and by my endless curiosity about what happens when different disciplines come together.

It started as a small studio, a collective of artists and craft designers (from carpet weavers to copper artisans, from painters to calligraphers), and even a few musicians. We came together to experiment and create environments that could make people feel, joy, calm, focus, even a sense of belonging. We weren't designing rooms; we were designing experiences.

That work later became the foundation of my bachelor's research, exploring how spatial design influences human emotion and well-being. Whether we were designing a workspace, a café, or a home, the question was always the same:

How can we design spaces that nurture human potential? The materials, textures, and lighting were just the medium. The real design was invisible, it lived in how people moved, interacted, and felt inside those spaces.

That was my first real experiment in transforming design into business. And this is where my journey in design-driven entrepreneurship truly began, long before I even thought of it as a term. It began at the intersection of design and entrepreneurship, where creativity becomes strategy, and where the act of building is as much about shaping human experience as it is about growing a business.

When people ask me what design-driven entrepreneurship means, I often tell them it's not a method, it's a mindset. It's what happens when design stops being the final layer that makes something look beautiful and becomes the driving force behind what makes it work. It's about seeing the world not as a set of problems to fix, but as a system to reimagine.

Design-driven entrepreneurship is what happens when you look at business like a designer, curious, empathetic, and relentlessly iterative. You stop asking, "How can I sell this?" and start asking, "How can I make this matter?" You move from creating products to creating meaning, from chasing growth to designing impact.

This approach blurs the lines between artistry and strategy, between purpose and profit. It's the space where innovation stops being an abstract word and becomes a lived practice. And once you start thinking this way — once you build not just to make, but to design — you can never go back.

Building for the Unknown

Let's face it—If you search "entrepreneurship" online, you'll tumble down a rabbit hole of contradictory advice. Some will tell you to manifest success under the full moon, while others will insist that sleep is a weakness and work is life. Between these extremes lies a space that's far more interesting, the place where creativity, logic, and caffeine quietly conspire to build something real.

Yet, there's still something missing in that picture. The conversations around entrepreneurship often focus on what to build and how to grow, but rarely on how to think, how to design ventures that are not only profitable but purposeful.

That's where Design-Driven Entrepreneurship (DDE) comes in. It begins with a simple impulse, the curiosity to look at a problem and think, there must be a better way. It's for those who see possibilities in constraints and meaning in the messy middle between vision and execution.

DDE isn't about following a playbook or checking boxes on a startup checklist. It's a practice of designing with intention, of shaping businesses as living systems that respond, evolve, and create value beyond profit. It's an approach that blends imagination with structure, empathy with analysis, and vision with the discipline to make it real.

So, what exactly is design-driven entrepreneurship? Business dressed up in trendy aesthetics or entrepreneurs wearing black turtlenecks? I hope not! To me, it's the moment when creativity becomes strategy, and ideas turn into systems that can move people, markets, and mindsets.

Here's the gist: While traditional entrepreneurship might start with "Let's build a better mousetrap," DDE begins with "Wait, do we even need a mousetrap? What if we design a way to live peacefully with mice instead?" It challenges assumptions, flips problems upside down, and sometimes even dissolves them altogether. DDE has the chance to be the entrepreneur's secret weapon against boring business plans and uninspired presentations

It's messy, experimental, and deeply human. And it just might be the most powerful way to build the future.

The Principles of DDE

1. Empathy is Your Superpower

In a world overflowing with noise, where everyone is bombarded by information, products, and ideas, it's worth asking: why would another app, another startup, another chair, even another book! - why would they matter?

Before I started writing this book, I asked myself that same question. There are millions of books out there. Many of them speak about design, entrepreneurship, or leadership, often by people far more experienced or famous than me. So why add another one to the pile?

But the more I thought about it, the clearer it became: we don't need more content, we need more guidance to help us connect what already exists, make sense of it, and turn it into something that actually works for us. So the difference isn't in the number of words we publish or the number of features we build, it's in how deeply those words or features resonate with someone's lived experience.

The same goes for business. In a market flooded with options, what makes one idea stand out isn't innovation alone, it's empathy. Because when everything starts to sound the same, the only thing that truly cuts through the noise is feeling understood.

That's what empathy does. It's the bridge between your intention and the world's need. It's what separates the founders who build products people tolerate from those who create solutions people can't live without.

Empathy means stepping into the shoes of your customers, employees, or even your critics. It's the ability to sense what people need before they can articulate it. Most businesses fail not because they lack technology or funding, but because they don't truly understand the human experience they're trying to improve.

Let's look at some numbers: as of 2025, there are over 9 million mobile apps across iOS and Android stores. That's 9 million attempts to make life "better." And yet, research shows that 90% of users abandon a new app within 30 days. Why? Because most of them solve a problem no one really has, or they solve it in a way no one wants.

Empathy flips that. It reminds you to stop asking, "How do I make people use my product?" and start asking, "How can I make something they actually need?"

That shift might sound small, but it's everything. It's the difference between designing another productivity app and creating something like Notion, which reimagined how people organize their minds, teams, and lives, by listening obsessively to how users actually think.

When I was studying architecture, I realized that even the design of a simple chair could transform someone's day — or their back pain. Empathy lives in those small, invisible choices that make a person feel seen, valued, and cared for.

And here's the thing: empathy isn't just emotional intelligence, it's strategic intelligence. It gives you access to insights no data dashboard can offer. It helps you anticipate behavior instead of reacting to it.

If you want to truly practice empathy, start by revisiting your own story. Go back to the moments when you ached to be understood — when you wished someone would simply get it. As the Persian philosopher and poet Rumi once wrote:

هرکسی از ظن خود شد یار من

از درون من نجست اسرار من

"Each person befriended me according to their own perception,
  yet none sought to know the secrets within me."

(The translation hardly captures the depth of it.)

Those moments are empathy gold. Harvest them. That's where your work can change lives.

2. Iteration is Key

Think of iteration like a toddler learning to walk: lots of stumbling, a fair amount of falling, but eventually, you're sprinting. In Norway there is a famous joke about how kids start skiing before they even learn to walk! No one would ever tell a toddler, "Oh sweetheart, stop trying, you're falling too much." Every wobble and crash is part of learning to move forward.

That's exactly how design-driven entrepreneurs should think. Iteration isn't failure, it's calibration. It's how you discover what actually works rather than what you hope will work. It's the process of listening, adjusting, and evolving until your creation begins to breathe on its own, until it fits into people's lives almost naturally.

Google famously launches hundreds of micro-experiments every year. Most of them fail quietly, but those "failures" generate learnings that feed into their next success. Gmail and AdSense, for example, were both side experiments that became multi-billion-dollar pillars of the company.

Take Canva, for instance. When it started, the idea was simple: democratize design. But the journey from idea to the platform we know today wasn't linear. Canva's founders ran through countless prototypes, messy beta versions, and clunky user flows before landing on something intuitive. They didn't chase perfection, they chased fit. Each redesign, each failed experiment, each piece of user feedback brought them closer to what we now call product–market fit, the magical point where what you've built perfectly aligns with what people actually need, use, and love. Even then, you will eventually be forced to pivot because, sorry to break it to you, but your customers are living beings, they evolve and so should your product and business..

In the startup world, many founders lose their way: they mistake traction for fit. They celebrate downloads, likes, or pilot users, early signals that often look exciting but mean little on their own. Traction is attention; fit is adoption. High traction looks impressive for a moment, but it doesn't last. Real innovation lives in the space between version 1.0 and version we stopped counting.

Here's the hard truth: a thousand people downloading your app doesn't mean you've built something meaningful. But a hundred people who keep coming back, week after week, because your product genuinely improves their lives, that's product-market fit. That's when your design has found its rhythm with real human behavior.

Let's be clear, investors love traction. It's visible, measurable, and makes for good slides. But retention is what separates a good pitch from a great product. It's easy to convince someone to try your app once; it's hard to make them come back week after week because it genuinely adds value to their life. Retention is proof that you've solved something meaningful. A design-driven entrepreneur doesn't chase traction metrics, they design for behavior. They ask:

- Why would someone use this twice?
- What makes it worth coming back to?
- What problem does it quietly erase from their life?

Iteration is what turns potential into proof. It's how you evolve from guessing what people want to understanding it. Each experiment, each redesign, each user conversation moves you closer to alignment between what you make and what the world truly needs. And that's when design stops being a phase, and becomes a philosophy.

3. Systems Thinking: Seeing the Invisible

No problem exists in isolation. Every decision you make, from hiring one person to changing your packaging, ripples through a larger system.

DDE forces you to zoom out and see the "butterfly effect" beyond a movie starring Ashton Kutcher. It's like switching from Google Maps' street view to satellite mode. You stop seeing individual points and start seeing the network, the invisible web of relationships, dependencies, and consequences that shape everything.

For example, when Starbucks redesigned its cup lids to eliminate plastic straws, it wasn't just a sustainability move. It forced an entire shift in their supply chain, manufacturing methods, and customer experience. That's systems thinking, understanding that every action in business exists within a larger ecosystem of people, resources, and impact.

When you start thinking this way, your decisions change. You don't just design a product, you design its afterlife, its footprint, its role in the world. You don't just create a hiring policy, you design the culture it will produce five years down the line.

Systems thinking is what turns founders into leaders, people who don't just build companies, but shape industries. In chapter 5, we will talk more about systemic thinking and design.

4. Beauty with Purpose

Yes, aesthetics matter — but DDE goes beyond surface beauty. It's not about making things pretty; it's about making them meaningful.

When beauty meets purpose, it stops being decoration and becomes design.

Apple's success wasn't built on sleek products alone. It was built on the philosophy that design is how something works, not just how it looks. Every curve, every sound, every animation was crafted to make users feel joy in the experience.

And the science backs this up: studies from the Design Management Institute show that design-led companies outperform the S&P 500 by more than 200% over a ten-year period.

Why? Because beauty — when done with purpose — creates emotional connection. It builds trust. It turns products into love stories.

Consider Dyson. They didn't just design vacuum cleaners, they redesigned the experience of cleaning itself. The visual transparency of their machines wasn't just for aesthetics; it was to let users see the engineering and understand the value they were paying for. That's beauty with purpose, form following meaning.

A Quick Reflection Exercise: Bringing DDE Into Your Own Business

If you're building something — a startup, a product, a brand — here's how to apply these four principles right now:

1. Empathy Check:
Ask five potential users about their biggest frustrations. Don't pitch. Just listen. Write down their words exactly as they say them.

2. Iterate Quickly:
Build a version of your idea that takes you one day, not one month. Test it with those same five users. Learn. Repeat.

3. Map the System:
Draw a quick sketch of your ecosystem: users, suppliers, investors, environment. What happens if one part changes? Who feels it?

4. Design for Meaning:
Ask yourself: If my product disappeared tomorrow, what would people actually miss about it? That's your design brief.

So Why is DDE Important?

Let's face it, our world is a mess. Climate change? Check. Economic disparity? Double check. Trying to figure out why your Wi-Fi keeps dropping during Zoom calls? Triple check. Add to that political instability, algorithm-driven polarization, unsustainable consumption, burnout disguised as productivity, and yes, even war being treated as a viable business model.

These are not simple problems. They demand more than spreadsheets, pitch decks, or the latest corporate buzzwords. They require creativity, resilience, and a willingness to color outside the lines, to think and act like a designer in a world that desperately needs redesigning.

Design-Driven Entrepreneurship (DDE) is essential because it helps us navigate this complexity without losing our sanity, or our sense of humor. It's about building businesses that are both profitable and purposeful, proving that you can, in fact, save the world and make payroll.

DDE is the antidote to the old way of doing business, the era when "innovation" was an afterthought and "design" meant "make it look cool." Instead, it reminds us that design isn't decoration; it's direction. It's not an accessory to business—it's the engine that drives it forward.

In the rest of this chapter, we'll explore the origins of DDE, the mindset it cultivates, and the tools you need to wield it effectively. We'll unpack why it's not just about thinking like a designer—it's about living like one: with curiosity, creativity, empathy, and a dash of audacity.

So, let's dive in—because you didn't pick up this book to settle for ordinary solutions. You're here to design extraordinary ones.

The Intersection of Design, Entrepreneurship, and Systemic Thinking

On the surface, design, entrepreneurship, and systemic thinking might seem like three distinct worlds, like a mismatched trio at a dinner party. Design is about creating with purpose; entrepreneurship is about turning ideas into impact; and systemic thinking is about seeing the big picture and understanding how all the pieces connect. But when you bring them together, they stop being separate fields, they become one powerful lens for reshaping the world.

Here's how they work: design gives us the tools to think creatively, entrepreneurship provides the drive to bring those ideas to life, and systemic thinking ensures we're not just solving symptoms but addressing root causes. It's a way of tackling complexity head-on, without getting stuck in the chaos.

For me, this intersection has always felt like home. Growing up in Isfahan, surrounded by breathtaking architecture and vibrant bazaars, I saw firsthand how design and commerce could shape communities. My father's work in construction and heavy engineering taught me that success isn't just about building things—it's about understanding the systems they exist within. My mother's work as a social entrepreneur showed me how empathy and creativity could transform lives.

This foundation stayed with me, even as I ventured into architecture school, then later into design. At the time, I didn't realize it, but every step was leading me toward this intersection of disciplines, a place where I could connect creativity with purpose and scale those ideas through thoughtful, systemic strategies.

I count myself lucky in this regard, grateful for the perspective I've gained, and aware of the responsibility that comes with it. So, let me keep sharing my story with you—and who knows, maybe one day, I'll get to hear yours and learn from it too.

Reimagining the World

Design school, beyond being a place to learn skills, was a place to unlearn boundaries. The studio was a playground for creativity, a testing ground where ideas were poked, stretched, and occasionally turned upside down. It was a space where "thinking outside the box" wasn't just encouraged—it was expected. Perfection didn't matter; exploration did. We didn't even have grades. All that mattered was you, and what you made of your journey into the unknown.

This ethos was embodied in exercises that encouraged students to push the limits of their imagination, like the deceptively simple task of coming up with "50 new ways to drink water."

At first glance, the assignment seemed absurd. Water is water, how many ways could there be to drink it? But the exercise wasn't about practicality. It was about breaking free from assumptions and seeing the ordinary in new extraordinary ways.

As ideas unfolded—from

- sipping water as steam to absorbing it through a wearable hydration patch
- Or Turning it into edible spheres and pop them like candy
- Or blending it with clouds of citrus mist and inhale the flavor.
- Or freezing it into intricate ice sculptures and let it melt into your cup.

—the exercise revealed how creativity thrives when unshackled from the need to be "right." The possibilities weren't limited by the water itself but by how far one could stretch their thinking.

This mindset of challenging the ordinary extended beyond the classroom. Another project required students to design prototypes that intentionally failed, showcasing how failure could expose blind spots and inspire innovation. These exercises weren't just creative warm-ups, they were lessons in resilience, curiosity, and the joy of iteration. They taught that creating something that lasts isn't about having all the answers; it's about asking the right questions and following them wherever they lead.

Seeing the World Sideways

To design is to look twice, to notice what everyone else walks past and ask, "Why does it have to be this way?" It's not about changing things for the sake of change; it's about seeing layers of possibility where others see routine. Designers don't accept the world at face value, they tilt their heads, squint a little, and realize that even the most ordinary things are built on choices that can be unmade and remade.

A designer's greatest tool isn't software or sketchbooks, it's perspective. Where most people see a broken system, a designer sees a prototype that hasn't been finished yet. Where others see chaos, they see a pattern waiting to emerge. This shift in perception turns frustration into fuel. Think about it: every great idea begins with someone being slightly dissatisfied with how things are.

Take a city bench. To most, it's just a place to sit. But a designer might wonder, what stories unfold on that bench each day? How does it shape the rhythm of the street? Could it collect solar energy to power nearby lights, or shift its shape to invite conversation? The power of perspective lies not in grand revolutions, but in the quiet courage to see potential where others see permanence.

When I was in architecture school in Iran, we took part in a collaboration course with the Architectural Association in London. The goal of the course was to design "urban machines" — that could mean vehicles, tools, pavilions, or any kind of spatial intervention capable of influencing people in what was called a supernormal urban environment.

Our site was Tajrish Square, one of the most crowded and chaotic places in Tehran. It's an intense urban node where seven streets collide, creating a whirlwind of motion and interaction. It's the kind of place where, no matter who you are or where you live in this province of over 14 million people, you'll probably pass through at least once a month. It's also a place of extremes, where the wealthy neighborhoods of north Tehran press up against working-class districts. It's where luxury SUVs park beside street vendors' carts, and where every social layer of the city brushes shoulders, often without even seeing each other. It's loud, colorful, overwhelming, and deeply human.

In this context, our task was deceptively simple: to design small-scale spatial objects like chairs or mini-pavilions that could shift how people experience that intense environment. Our group ended up designing a movable, semi-private space built from very basic materials. It was essentially a standing, semi-transparent wall with a moiré effect that people could easily move.

The idea was to give individuals or small groups a way to carve out a moment of calm within the chaos — not by isolating themselves completely, but by slightly reframing their experience of the space.

These mobile walls could be placed near the fixed seating in the square, turning those public benches into something a bit more personal, something that gave a sense of partial enclosure, a little buffer from the flow of the crowd. It let people just be, even in the middle of one of the busiest intersections in the city. That project turned out to be one of our most successful interventions.

Living with a designer's lens means living with constant awareness. The way a line curves, how people move through space, how a service makes someone feel—it's all data, waiting to be reimagined. It's walking into a room and noticing not just what's there, but what could be. It's understanding that the world isn't fixed—it's a draft.

This isn't limited to the design studio. Entrepreneurs, teachers, doctors, and activists, all can benefit from this way of seeing. The designer's mindset is really a human mindset at its best: curious, observant, and restless enough to believe that things can always be better.

Perspective, after all, is the birthplace of innovation. Once you learn to look sideways at the world, you stop accepting limits, and start designing your way past them.

The Designer's Mindset in Entrepreneurship

I once came across a student project that has stayed with me for years—simple, poetic, and profoundly revealing. In a bustling urban square, students poured water-based paint across the ground, allowing passersby to unknowingly pick up pigment on their shoes. With each step, pause, or turn, people left colorful footprints behind, gradually transforming the space. From a nearby tower, the students filmed the unfolding patterns as movement accumulated over hours and days.

What began as scattered and chaotic marks slowly revealed an emergent logic. Certain paths became densely layered where people consistently walked; other areas remained almost untouched. Without realizing it, every pedestrian became a co-creator of a living map, a record of how the space was actually used, as opposed to how it was designed to be used.

That project revealed the invisible systems that shape human behavior. Footprints traced shortcuts no one was meant to take, spots where people paused to meet, or edges where the built environment resisted the natural flow. And when the rain came, it washed the traces away, leaving only faint ghosts of movement, but the insight remained.

This experience was part of shaping how I think about design and innovation. What those students captured wasn't just movement; it was the relationship between people and systems, between behavior and space. It made me realize that the best design, and, by extension, the most impactful entrepreneurship, is not about imposing order but about revealing and responding to existing patterns. It's about learning to see the unseen, listening to what the environment is already telling us, and designing with that knowledge in mind.

Design-driven entrepreneurship (DDE) operates on this same principle. It embraces complexity instead of simplifying it, mapping systems in motion and using empathy, experimentation, and iteration to find meaning within them. Just as that painted square became a metaphor for emergent behavior, markets and companies evolve through the small, often unconscious choices of people interacting with them.

The most transformative ventures emerge not from improving existing models, but from reimagining them altogether. Airbnb didn't ask how to make hotels better; it asked whether homes could become spaces of hospitality. Tesla didn't settle for efficient electric cars, it asked how they could be exhilarating. These shifts weren't born from certainty, but from curiosity and a willingness to dwell in ambiguity.

That's what a designer's mindset brings to entrepreneurship. It teaches us to reframe problems, to see interdependencies, and to design not just for users, but for systems, understanding how decisions about materials, manufacturing, distribution, or disposal ripple across economies, cultures, and ecosystems.

DDE encourages us to zoom out and recognize that no business operates in isolation. It helps us find leverage points in complex systems—linking user needs with systemic challenges and long-term impact. In doing so, it turns complexity from a constraint into a source of innovation.

But perhaps the most powerful aspect of this mindset is how it responds to uncertainty. Designers don't avoid ambiguity, they lean into it. They treat confusion as fertile ground for invention and treat setbacks as prototypes for new ideas. Whether rethinking something as basic as public seating or confronting climate change, design-driven thinkers envision what could be, not just what is.

In a world shaped by interconnected crises, ecological, social, technological, DDE offers more than a method. It offers a way of seeing. It teaches us that thriving in complexity isn't about having all the answers; it's about asking better questions and designing our way forward with empathy, intention, and imagination.

Exercises:

1. Reverse Empathy Test: Be the Object

Instead of observing someone else, become the object of their interaction. Pretend you're a door, a chair, or even a piece of software. What would it feel like to be used or misused? Where would you feel strain, neglect, or appreciation?

Twist: Write a diary entry from the perspective of the object or system after a "day's work." What did you learn?

2. The "What If Everything Changed?" Game

Pick an ordinary activity, like grocery shopping or driving, and imagine the rules of the world have shifted:
- What if gravity doubled?
- What if all written language disappeared?
- What if humans had three arms?

Design a solution for these new realities.

Bonus: Share your wildest idea with a friend and see how they'd iterate on it.

3. Random Mashup Challenge

Grab two completely unrelated objects or concepts (e.g., a teapot and a smartphone). Now design something that blends their functions.

Example: A teapot that brews tea and sends text reminders when your tea is ready.

Twist: Add a third object into the mix for extra chaos and creativity!

4. Human Library: Borrow a Life

Spend an hour with someone whose daily life is completely different from yours, an artist, a mechanic, a nurse. Ask them about their challenges, routines, and moments of joy.

Challenge: Design a tool, system, or service that would make their day easier or more fulfilling.

Bonus: Present your idea to them and get their feedback.

5. Future Mapping Exercise

Imagine it's 50 years from now, and a product or service you use every day no longer exists. Why did it disappear? What replaced it?

Outcome: Design its replacement, something innovative, ethical, and future-ready.

6. Build a World from One Object

Take a random object near you (a pen, a pair of glasses, a mug) and design an entire fictional world where this object is central to daily life. How would people use it? What new rituals or industries might emerge?

Bonus: Write a short story about a character in this world and how the object shapes their life.

7. The Systems Hack

Pick a broken system you interact with, maybe it's your commute, healthcare, or even your email inbox. Map out its pain points and bottlenecks. Now reimagine it:

• What would a frictionless version look like?
• What other systems would it influence if redesigned?

Action Step: Implement one small fix and track its impact.

14. The Everyday Prototype

Take one small frustration in your life and design a quick prototype to solve it. Use whatever materials are at hand—paper, tape, string, or even digital tools.

Twist: Ask a friend to test your prototype and tell you what works and what doesn't.

These exercises invite you to see the world with fresh eyes, to explore curiosity, and to discover how the ordinary can turn extraordinary. Grab a notebook, jump in, and let your imagination lead the way, just keep asking, "What if?"

Chapter 4:
Tea, Wine, and Trust

My grandfather always told me:

"Business is about people, Nilu. And people are their cultures."

I didn't fully grasp the depth of his words until I left Iran. Only then, moving from country to country, did they return to me again and again, like a compass.

In Iran, I grew up in bazaars where business didn't begin with contracts but with conversations over tea. Trust and reputation were the real currencies, and relationships were the foundation of every exchange. Messy at times, too informal perhaps, but deeply human.

Then came Norway. I still remember the night I had to decide about studying abroad.

My father looked at me and said:

"Nilu, look at the history of the Middle East over the past decades. You can hardly find a single day without conflict. And that means not even a single day when nations could look beyond survival. Go to a country that has had the privilege of stability, one that has learned from everyone else's mistakes, and had the time to embed those lessons into its society. Go there, and learn from their mistakes."

His words struck me like lightning. That night, I chose Norway. And when I arrived, everything ran on systems and structures. Meetings were short, decisions transparent, equality embedded in the way people worked together. It looked different, but in principle, only the tea from the bazaars was replaced by a glass of wine—or, more often, free beer. The spirit of connection was the same, only wrapped in a different ritual.

The biggest difference, though, was me. An immigrant from Iran, a place many saw as more unknown than a black hole, with big, dark eyes that were not immediately trusted. Every move meant starting from scratch. I had to decode cultural cues and prove myself in rooms where I was often the outsider.

However, the saving grace was design and moving across various countries for work or studies. As a designer, I knew how to read, navigate, and gently nudge systems to carve out a place in every crowd. And on that note, Denmark gave me a little more slack. There, design wasn't just an industry, it was a cultural backbone. From the bicycle lanes threading through cities to the way public spaces were formed, dignity, simplicity, and sustainability were woven into daily life. It felt like design was our universal language regardless of our different professions as people. Denmark's strong design tradition made me feel, perhaps for the first time, a little more at home. But by then, I had also gotten better at "playing the man."

Then came Kenya, where business pulsed with ingenuity. Scarcity didn't limit, it fueled creativity. Nothing was wasted; everything could be reimagined and repurposed. The joy of nothing else could compare to the sense of freedom that I felt there.

France added another dimension: business as elegance, where every detail carried weight. From Parisian cafés to artisanal workshops, every interaction was carefully crafted, blending aesthetics and intention. Business was treated like an art and a performance, where you earned trust only if you were memorable through your sense of refinement, care, and subtle understanding of human sensibilities.

Italy, on the other hand, taught me about passion in business, the way artistry and craftsmanship were inseparable from commerce. Whether it was furniture, food, or fashion, business there was an act of cultural expression.

Spain showed me the power of rhythm and community. Long lunches, late-night talks, and the blending of work with life were not inefficiencies, they were investments in trust. Business there wasn't rushed; it was nourished, like a good meal shared among friends.

Greece blended resilience with dialogue and community, reminding me that business could be cultural, philosophical, and deeply social all at once.

Germany challenged me in another way. Precision and order ruled not just design, but also business. Every process had a system, every decision a protocol. At first, I struggled with the rigidity, but soon I realized that discipline creates trust just as much as improvisation does, it just wears a different mask.

Lithuania, by contrast, felt more like rediscovering roots. A place small in scale but big in spirit, where entrepreneurship was carried by ambition and hunger to prove oneself on the global stage. There I saw how resilience and community pride could drive innovation just as strongly as systems or elegance.

Each country had its own rhythm. Norway's trust in systems was nothing like Kenya's trust in improvisation. France's flair was nothing like Denmark's quiet pragmatism. Germany's discipline was nothing like Lithuania's scrappy ambition. Spain's warmth was nothing like Italy's fiery artistry. And yet, beneath these differences, I noticed the same heartbeat:

business everywhere began with people. And wherever people were, trust was the common currency. Without it, no deal, no innovation, no collaboration could survive.

Now, with an organization spread across 20 countries, I live and work like a nomad entrepreneur, moving between worlds, weaving them together. I've learned that business and innovation isn't about imposing solutions. It's about honoring cultures, building bridges, and designing with people rather than for them. Each culture offers its own lens, but trust is the thread that stitches them all together.

That's where true innovation lives: in embracing culture as the raw material of design, and design as the tool that transforms business into something deeply human.

Business without people is empty.
Design without context is shallow.
And entrepreneurship without empathy is fragile.

Moving to a new country is often described as an adventure, but to me, it felt more like stepping into a kaleidoscope, familiar shapes rearranged into something completely new. I left Iran to explore a world far beyond what I knew. Every step since has been a leap into the unknown.

Leaving meant letting go, of comfort, of certainty, of the limits I thought I had. I moved, built, succeeded, failed, learned, struggled, created, doubted, and kept going. Through it all, I loved, cared, connected, and never stopped chasing the extraordinary, whether possible or not.

In Norway, the first thing I noticed was the silence. Not an eerie silence, but one that felt intentional, like the pause between two carefully chosen words. It was such a contrast to the life I had left behind in Iran, where every corner of every street seemed to hum with stories. That silence forced me to listen differently, not just to the world around me, but to the systems beneath it.

This experience shaped the way I see entrepreneurship. Because, just like moving to a new country, building something new means stepping into the unknown. Most founders I've met, and I've been there too, rush headfirst into building the next big thing, fixated on the product, the pitch deck, the metrics, the forecasts. The screens glow late into the night with code, designs, and financial models, as if enough refinement will guarantee impact.

And to be fair, this is what most accelerators and incubators teach us to do. They're brilliant at giving founders the tools to raise capital, calculate KPIs, and refine business models. But there's a trap hidden in this approach: we end up optimizing for spreadsheets and growth curves while becoming disconnected from the very people we set out to serve. We get "blocked behind our computers," missing the subtle signals of trust, culture, and behavior that decide whether a business will live or die.

The startup ecosystem rewards speed, visibility, and traction. But business is not just numbers, it's profoundly human. Relationships are the scaffolding of every deal, every adoption, every pivot. Customers buy from people they trust. Teams thrive when their leaders understand their motivations. Investors back founders they believe in, not just products they think can scale.

Ignoring this human dimension is why so many technically brilliant startups fail. They deliver functional solutions but remain disconnected, unmemorable, invisible to the people they were meant to serve.

Design-driven entrepreneurship is an antidote to this problem. It asks founders to step out from behind their screens and into the world. To observe, empathize, and immerse themselves in the lives of the people they hope to reach. It reveals patterns that no data dashboard can show you, how trust is built, how decisions are really made, what people value when no one is watching.

A single well-designed interaction, a conversation that listens more than it talks, a product feature that addresses an unspoken need, these can change everything.

This approach doesn't reject business discipline; it balances it. Yes, use your incubator frameworks, build your models, measure your KPIs, but filter them through a human lens. Treat your startup as a living system to be nurtured, not just an engine to be scaled.

When founders do this, they stop simply implementing plans and start co-creating ecosystems of trust and value. And when investors look beyond the numbers, seeking not just traction but relational intelligence, cultural awareness, and adaptability, they find ventures that last, not just ones that grow fast.

The biggest blind spot in entrepreneurship is not technology, not marketing, not capital. It's the human element. Those who neglect it stay trapped behind their screens, chasing numbers and building products that never resonate. Those who embrace it unlock something far richer: ventures that thrive within human systems, businesses that matter, and success that is measured not just by profit, but by the impact they leave behind.

Adapting to New Environments and Finding Opportunities in Complexity

Entering a new country or industry often feels like being dropped into a maze where the rules are unwritten and the exits are hidden. At first, it feels like you are at a disadvantage, but in time, you begin to notice patterns that locals may overlook because they've become too accustomed to the system to see it clearly. This "outsider perspective" can be an advantage if you are willing to listen, to map the system, and to experiment with how you move within it.

The world rarely presents itself in neat, well-labeled boxes. Instead, it throws us into unpredictable, overlapping systems where markets shift overnight, technologies disrupt entire industries, and cultures collide in ways that force us to question what we thought we knew.

The best entrepreneurs, designers, and innovators I've met didn't succeed because the path was clear. They succeeded because they were willing to move forward even when the map was missing, trusting that clarity would emerge through action.

Take Airbnb. In the early days, it wasn't a polished business model — it was two founders renting out air mattresses in their apartment to make rent. That was a chaotic, imperfect solution to a personal problem, but they noticed something hidden in the noise: a pattern of people craving local, affordable, authentic travel experiences. Instead of waiting for certainty, they built iteratively in the middle of uncertainty. They didn't eliminate complexity — they leaned into it and turned it into an industry-shifting opportunity.

Or think about SpaceX. When Elon Musk announced he wanted to send reusable rockets into orbit, the aerospace industry considered it almost laughable. The complexity of rocket science was a barrier even for governments, let alone a scrappy private company. But by breaking the problem into smaller, solvable pieces — building, testing, failing, iterating — they reduced the complexity into actionable steps. Each crash landing wasn't the end but another data point, another insight into how to get closer to a reusable rocket. Complexity became their competitive advantage because they were willing to keep showing up when others stopped.

In design, we see this every day. When IDEO redesigned the patient experience for Kaiser Permanente, they didn't just improve a few hospital forms or paint the waiting rooms a different color. They immersed themselves in the system, shadowing doctors, nurses, and patients to uncover hidden friction points. They found that nurses were spending hours each shift just tracking down missing information about their patients. By reimagining shift-change protocols and information handoffs, IDEO helped reduce medical errors and improve patient satisfaction — not by simplifying the environment but by embracing its complexity and finding leverage points for change.[23]

This is exactly what systemic design is built for, untangling complexity without oversimplifying it. In my time studying systemic design, one of the most memorable projects was when we were tasked with redesigning democracy. Yes, democracy itself, not a single campaign, not a single policy, but the very idea of how power, representation, and participation function in society.

At first, the assignment felt overwhelming. Democracy was something we took for granted as a given, a fixed system. But systemic design asked us to break it apart, map its actors and interactions, and look at the hidden feedback loops that shaped the outcomes we see in the world. We had to ask radical questions:

- What if democracy wasn't about majority rule but about collective intelligence?
- What if representation wasn't limited to people but extended to nature, future generations, or even artificial intelligence?
- What if participation wasn't episodic—every four years at a ballot box—but continuous, woven into everyday life?

Those sessions weren't just theoretical debates — they were creative laboratories. We sketched systems, mapped power flows, and prototyped alternative ways of structuring civic life.

And this wasn't just an academic exercise. Around the world, others are doing this work in real time. Take Brazil's participatory budgeting movement — where citizens gather in assemblies to directly decide how a portion of municipal budgets should be spent. Or Taiwan's vTaiwan project, where citizens, policymakers, and experts collaborate online to debate and co-create legislation. These systemic design efforts don't just "fix" democracy; they reimagine it for a networked, fast-moving world.

The process taught me that complexity isn't a wall to be scaled, it's a network to be understood. And once you understand it, you can intervene more wisely, finding leverage points where small, intentional changes create disproportionate impact.

Complexity is where the hidden opportunities live. It's where you find unmet needs, misaligned incentives, and broken processes waiting to be reimagined. But you can only find them if you're willing to stay present in the discomfort — to sit in the silence long enough to hear what's really happening, to observe the patterns before rushing to solve them.

The key is reframing complexity as an invitation, not a threat. When others see a mess and back away, you step forward. When others are paralyzed by uncertainty, you move, even if it's a small step. When others search for the perfect answer, you search for the better question.

Because here's the truth: the world doesn't get simpler. Business doesn't get simpler. Systems don't get simpler. But we can get better at seeing them, understanding them, and working with them — like a surfer who learns not to fight the ocean but to ride the waves it gives.

And that's where design and entrepreneurship intersect most powerfully: at the point where complexity stops being a barrier and becomes a canvas.

Exercise: Design Across Cultures

These exercises are not just warm-ups; they're a chance to step into the "beautiful chaos" of cultural diversity and turn it into design fuel.

1. Culture Remix Challenge

Pick an everyday ritual (like commuting, coffee breaks, team meetings). Research how this ritual happens in two vastly different countries. Now mash them together: what would a hybrid version look like? Could it create more connection, joy, or efficiency? Sketch it, storyboard it, or write a scenario.

2. The Outsider's Eye

Spend one afternoon pretending you just arrived from another planet. Observe a public place—a café, a library, a supermarket—and document every small thing that feels odd or could be improved. Then redesign the experience for a first-timer so that it feels more inclusive, human, and intuitive.

3. The Trust Map

Pick a project or relationship you're working on right now and draw a "trust map." Who are the key players? How strong is the trust between them? Where are the gaps? Now, brainstorm 3 concrete actions you could take to strengthen trust in the weakest links.

This is the work of a design-driven entrepreneur—turning friction into fuel, complexity into clarity, and diversity into design breakthroughs. These exercises are not just "homework," they're small experiments to shift how you see the world. The more you practice, the more natural it becomes to find opportunity in the unexpected.

Next, we'll explore how design becomes a driver for innovation, not just within products or services, but in reimagining entire systems. For now, let yourself sit in the messiness—it's where the best ideas (and the best leaders) are born.

Chapter 5:
Dancing With The System

When I finished my bachelor's degree in architecture in Iran, I wrapped it up with a massive project, several thousand square meters of built space. It was a creativity center, an ambitious hybrid that blended a Fab Lab, an incubator, an coworking space, and public workshops. At its core, it was shaped by the ideas I'd explored in my thesis, how spatial design and perception could actively support and nudge creativity. It was urban, but deeply local. It was large in scale, layered in purpose, and to me, it felt like the first real-world embodiment of the ideas that would later grow into the foundation of this book.

Just a couple of months after completing that project, I found myself in a completely different world, sitting in a design school in Norway, on the very first day of class. The task we were given was deceptively simple: rethink a flashlight. From a multi-thousand-square-meter creativity hub to a handheld object that needed to sit comfortably in the palm of my hand. My mind nearly short-circuited.

Everything shifted in that moment. In architecture, the word "concept" carried a certain weight, tied to space, structure, context. But here, in product design, it meant something entirely different, tactile, intimate, precise. I had to start over. I had to study my own hand, how it moved, how it gripped, how it communicated with an object. The flashlight wasn't just a design exercise; it became a crash course in scale, in sensitivity, in noticing.

Looking back, I now realize that was the moment when my mind started learning how to move between vastly different scales. From macro environments that spanned entire city blocks, to micro gestures contained within a single finger's motion—and everything in between. That shift in perspective, that flexibility, became the most valuable tool I could have developed.

Later, I came to understand that this way of thinking—this ability to zoom in and out seamlessly—is at the heart of systemic design. It's not just about solving one problem at one scale. It's about navigating the whole spectrum, understanding how a change in one small component can ripple out across an entire system. That flashlight changed more than my approach to design, it rewired how I think.

Complex problems are everywhere. They're the messy, interconnected challenges that resist simple solutions, fragmented industries, inefficient systems, and societal issues that defy quick fixes. These problems don't live in isolation, and neither can their solutions. That's where systemic design comes in.

Systemic design, just like design itself, is more than a methodology; it's a mindset. It's about zooming out to see the bigger picture while keeping the people at the heart of the system in focus. It's the ability to connect dots others don't see, to navigate and visualize complexity without getting lost in it, and to design solutions that create lasting impact.

My first introduction to systemic design was under the guidance of Prof. Birger Svaldson, a pioneer in the field and author of book "Designing Complexity". His approach wasn't about simplifying complexity—it was about embracing it, learning to see the patterns, and using them to design interventions that work. It was like being handed a map to a world I didn't know existed, one where problems weren't obstacles but opportunities to create meaningful change.

In this chapter, we'll explore the principles and tools of systemic design, share real-world examples of its transformative power, and uncover how this approach has reshaped industries. By the end, you'll see that complexity isn't something to fear. In fact, the most challenging problems often hold the most extraordinary opportunities.

But before we continue, I have an exercise for you:

MAP YOURSELF

Grab a large blank sheet of paper. Big enough that it feels slightly intimidating.

Now, write this phrase in the center: "Me, right now." That's your starting point. That's your anchor.

Your task is to map yourself, not your resume, not your timeline, not what others see, but you. The way you are, think, move, love, resist, dream, adapt, fight, fail, heal.

You can include places, people, patterns, roles you've played, turning points, things you've outgrown, things you're moving toward. Use shapes, colors, lines, keywords, whatever makes sense to you.

There's no right way to do this. There's just the way YOU do it.

Don't overthink it. Start somewhere, anywhere. Let one memory or piece of yourself lead to the next.

This map won't look like anyone else's. And that's exactly the point.

The First Blueprint Of Your Impact, Is YOU

How was the exercise?

Well, not very easy I believe but rather joyful! Wasn´t it?

This is what Birger put us through first day of the Systemic Design course!

It caught me completely off guard. He looked at me and said,

"Nilu, map yourself."

I just stared at him. Map myself? What does that even mean?

Now, by this point in the book, you've probably gathered that I haven't exactly followed a clean, straight line in life. I haven't been the most conventional student, the easiest collaborator, or someone who just fits neatly into categories. My path has been... tangled, messy, full of detours and contradictions.

And yet, there I was, with Birger handing me a huge blank sheet of white paper and repeating, calmly, "Map yourself."

I didn't know where to begin. Not even a clue. Not because I didn't have stories or experiences, but because I didn't know how to frame them. What counted as "me"? Was it geography? People? Projects? Feelings? Failures? skills? I sat there for a long while, completely stuck.

But here's the thing: that moment became a turning point in me. That's when I realized that if I don't draw that map, I may never truly see where I am, or who I've become. Because if you don't make sense of who you are, you'll end up building things that try to make sense of you.

You'll pour your confusion, your contradictions, your unfinished questions into the work, hoping the things you create will explain what you haven't yet understood about yourself. But that's only a projection.

Mapping yourself is the first act of design. It's how you build from clarity, not from chaos.

And as an entrepreneur, you're not just building a product, you're building from your life. You're pouring everything into it: your time, your energy, your resources, your mental and physical health, your relationships, your identity. You sacrifice and stretch and invest every part of yourself in the hope that what you're building will help the world, maybe even save it.

But if you don't know who you are, who's doing the building, who needs saving first—then what exactly are you offering? You can't save the world if you're lost inside yourself. Or at the very least, if you haven't tried to make sense of who you are alongside the thing you're trying to build.

That's why this exercise matters. And no, this map isn't a one-time assignment. Just like your customers change, your market evolves, your team adapts, you do too. You iterate. You shift. You're a living, complex system constantly manifesting something new.

Being able to map yourself—again and again—isn't just a personal ritual. It's a strategic necessity. Because the way you show up in your work shapes the kind of impact you can have. How well you understand yourself will quietly, but deeply, influence how you end up trying to save the world.

Tools and Principles for Systemic Design

Designing for complexity goes beyond understanding the problem, it's about understanding the system that creates the problem. Systemic design is the practice of addressing complex challenges by seeing them as interrelated, dynamic systems. It blends the analytical depth of systems thinking with the generative power of design. It helps us not only respond to issues, but to reshape entire ecosystems through curiosity, collaboration, and action.

Systemic design works best when it's grounded in principles and powered by tools, methods that help us see patterns, listen to people, and navigate complexity with clarity.

Core Principles of Systemic Design

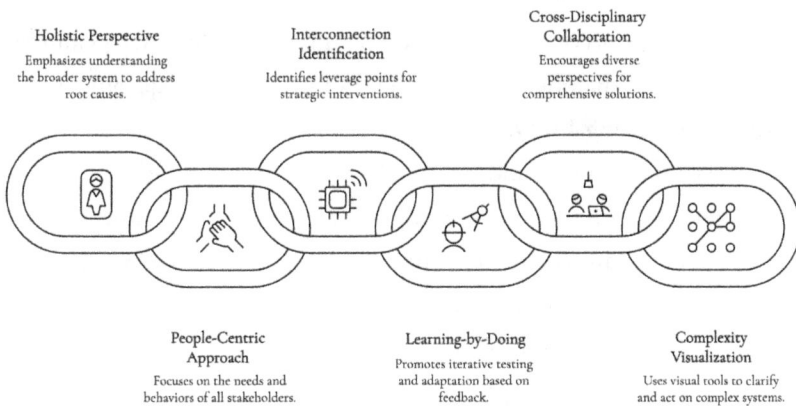

Holistic Perspective
Emphasizes understanding the broader system to address root causes.

Interconnection Identification
Identifies leverage points for strategic interventions.

Cross-Disciplinary Collaboration
Encourages diverse perspectives for comprehensive solutions.

People-Centric Approach
Focuses on the needs and behaviors of all stakeholders.

Learning-by-Doing
Promotes iterative testing and adaptation based on feedback.

Complexity Visualization
Uses visual tools to clarify and act on complex systems.

1. Take a Holistic Perspective

Systemic design begins with zooming out. Rather than fixating on isolated pain points, it explores the broader system to understand how elements influence one another. This big-picture perspective ensures that you're addressing root causes rather than surface-level symptoms.

Example: In healthcare, you wouldn't just optimize one department. You'd explore how administrative workflows, staff communication, patient journeys, and policy constraints interact across the entire system.

2. Focus on People, Within Their Context

Systemic design keeps people at the heart of the process—not just users, but every stakeholder touched by the system. It considers needs, behaviors, and environments together.

Example: When redesigning a public transportation system, you're not just designing for riders, you're also involving operators, city planners, policymakers, and service staff. Each viewpoint is essential to making the system work as a whole.

3. Identify Interconnections and Leverage Points

Most systemic problems don't come from one thing going wrong. They emerge from interactions, frictions, and feedback loops between many parts. Systemic design identifies leverage points, the small, strategic places where interventions can create outsized impacts.

Example: In the construction industry, improving how teams communicate, by redesigning shared tools or workflows, can significantly reduce delays and budget overruns, even more than hiring more labor or buying better equipment.

4. Embrace Learning-by-Doing

Complex systems evolve, and so should your solutions. Systemic design is inherently iterative. You test, observe, adjust, and repeat. It's not about perfection upfront, it's about adaptive progress informed by real-world feedback.

Prototyping, co-testing ideas with users, and embracing failure as data are essential elements of this mindset.

5. Collaborate Across Disciplines

No one discipline holds all the answers. Systemic design thrives on diversity of thought. By bringing together designers, engineers, scientists, business strategists, and community members, you allow for layered perspectives that lead to deeper insights and more resilient solutions.

6. Visualize Complexity

Seeing complexity makes it actionable. Tools like system maps, empathy maps, and GIGA-mapping transform abstract interconnections into visual stories that teams can understand, share, and act on. These tools help turn confusion into clarity and support collective sense-making.

Tools That Turn Systemic Thinking Into Systemic Action

System Maps: Visualizing the Whole

System maps are the backbone of systemic design. They offer a bird's-eye view of the system, allowing you to trace relationships, feedback loops, bottlenecks, and unseen influences. They make invisible structures visible.

How to Create a System Map:

- Define the System: What's inside the boundaries? What's outside? Be explicit about your scope.
- List the Components: Identify all relevant actors, processes, technologies, resources, regulations, and goals.
- Draw Relationships: Use arrows and lines to show flows, influences, conflicts, or dependencies between elements.
- Analyze Patterns: Look for loops, pain points, or leverage points where small changes could lead to systemic impact.

System maps are not static, they evolve as your understanding deepens. Use them as living documents to guide exploration, conversations, and iteration.

Empathy Maps: Understanding the Human Layer

Empathy maps shift the focus from abstract systems to lived experience. They help you get into the mindset of users or stakeholders, capturing not just what they do, but what they feel, fear, and hope for.

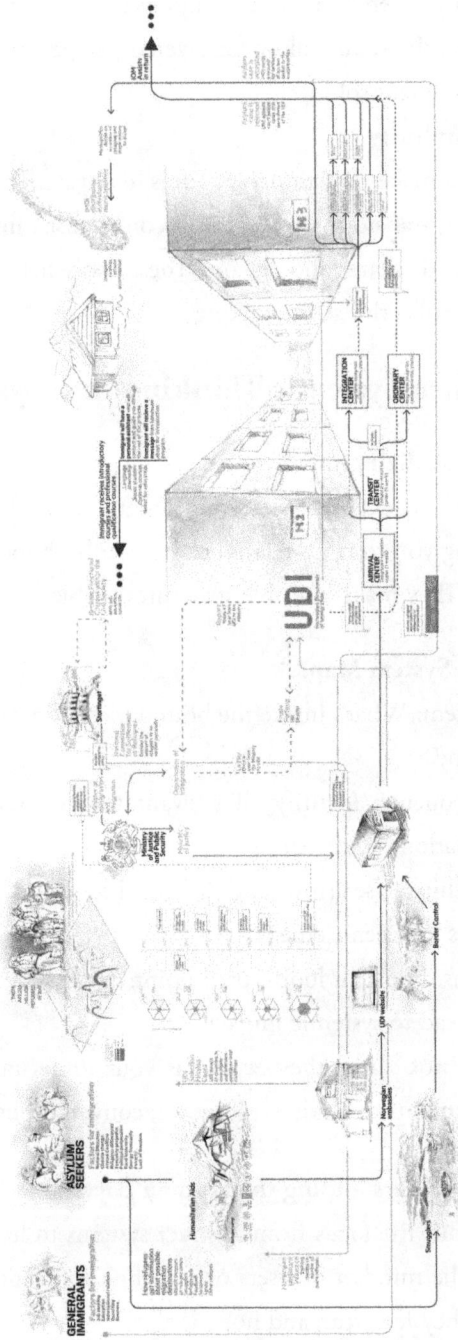

The "Asylum Journey to Norway" Giga Map! 3 meters long and 1.2 meters high! Don't even try to read it, but look at it as an example.

How to Use an Empathy Map

- Start with a Persona: Choose a real or representative user or stakeholder.
- Divide the Map into Quadrants:
    What do they see? (Their environment, influences, barriers)
    What do they hear? (Feedback, conversations, cultural narratives)
    What do they think and feel? (Motivations, fears, emotions)
    What do they say and do? (Actions, expressions, behaviors)
- Extract Insights: Use the map to surface unspoken needs, conflicting motivations, or misalignments between experience and intent.

Empathy maps bring emotional and social context into systems work, ensuring that solutions don't just work on paper, but resonate with real people.

Participatory Design: Designing With, Not For

Complex systems can't be redesigned from the top down. Participatory design brings stakeholders into the creative process. It acknowledges that those who live within the system hold critical insight—and must have a voice in shaping its future.

How to Facilitate Participatory Design:

- Co-Define the Problem: Don't arrive with answers. Start with questions, and shape the design brief together.
- Gather Diverse Stakeholders: Include users, policy makers, frontline workers, marginalized voices, domain experts, anyone impacted by or influencing the system.
- Engage with Collaborative Tools: Use co-creation sessions, storytelling, journey mapping, role-playing, and low-fi prototyping.
- Document and Integrate Feedback: Ensure contributions don't end up on the wall, they feed back into real decisions and iterations.

Participatory design builds trust, increases solution adoption, and unlocks knowledge you can't access from the outside.

Bringing It All Together

- These tools are powerful on their own—but transformative when used together:
- System maps reveal the structural and systemic patterns behind a problem.
- Empathy maps bring in the emotional and social realities of the people within that system.
- Participatory design ensures those people have agency in shaping the solutions that affect them.

Together, they form the backbone of systemic design, helping you navigate complexity not just with logic, but with humility and collaboration.

Whether you're tackling global sustainability, rethinking public services, or building an inclusive startup, these tools help you move from isolated fixes to integrated change. They don't just help you think systemically, they empower you to act systemically.

Systemic design is a framework, and a commitment to see the whole, to include the parts, and to design in ways that honor complexity rather than run away from it.

Applications of Systemic Design
Solving Fragmentation in Industries

Systemic design has been applied across various industries, transforming how they function by addressing their most entrenched challenges. Its strength lies in its ability to work across silos, integrate perspectives, and redesign systems from the inside out. Below I give you some examples.

Healthcare

Systemic Design mixed with Service Design reimagines the patient journey, addressing inefficiencies and improving care. By mapping patient interactions with doctors, nurses, and administrative systems, healthcare providers have created processes that prioritize both patient experience and operational efficiency.

Example: The Mayo Clinic's Center for Innovation applies systemic design to reimagine patient care by integrating experience mapping, ethnographic research, and service prototyping. They've restructured physical environments, appointment scheduling, and doctor-patient communication to better align with patient needs, reducing wait times and improving satisfaction.

Construction

The construction industry is notoriously fragmented, with architects, engineers, and contractors working in silos, causing delays, inefficiencies, and miscommunication. That was the challenge we set out to solve with Birdflocks, a Norway-based startup I co-founded with fellow architects. Our goal wasn't just to digitize workflows but to redesign collaboration itself.

Using systemic design, we mapped the entire ecosystem, identified bottlenecks, and united stakeholders through co-creation workshops to build a shared purpose. What emerged was meant to be more than a platform, it was about creating a mindset shift. Birdflocks became a living example of Design-Driven Entrepreneurship: iterative, collaborative, and systemic. We pivoted repeatedly to stay relevant in an industry where most startups targeted small problems, while we aimed to transform the system as a whole. It was complex, demanding, and often hard to explain, but our research revealed what the industry truly needed, and the team remains committed to responding to it.

A more established example of systemic design in construction is the Integrated Project Delivery (IPD) model which is used in projects like the UCSF Medical Center in San Francisco. It aligns all key players—clients, designers, builders— under a single contract and uses shared tools like BIM (Building Information Modeling) to collaboratively solve problems in real time, drastically reducing delays and budget blowouts.

Finance

Banks and fintech companies have used systemic design to transform rigid, siloed institutions into more responsive, human-centered ecosystems. By analyzing customer journeys and aligning internal departments, they've improved both digital experiences and overall customer satisfaction.

Example: Monzo, a UK-based digital bank, has built its entire service around systemic design principles. Instead of separate banking functions operating in isolation, Monzo developed transparent, user-centric systems that integrate customer support, budgeting tools, and real-time spending data. This redesign not only improved the customer experience but also reshaped internal workflows and culture. It broke down silos by building cross-functional teams with more cohesive operations and embodied iterative improvement through constant testing and user feedback.

Education

Schools and educational institutions are using systemic design to create adaptive, inclusive learning environments. By viewing students, teachers, administrators, parents, and technology as interconnected parts of a broader system, they've redesigned curricula, space, and pedagogy.

Example: High Tech High in San Diego applies systemic design to radically reimagine K-12 education. Interdisciplinary teams of educators design project-based learning experiences, while students co-create projects rooted in real-world challenges. Feedback loops between students, teachers, and community partners ensure the curriculum evolves with changing needs.[24]

Sustainability

Environmental challenges are by definition systemic. Circular economy initiatives use systemic design to rethink entire value chains, from sourcing and manufacturing to disposal and reuse.

Example: Interface, a global carpet tile manufacturer, adopted systemic design through its Mission Zero and Climate Take Back programs. By mapping its supply chain, production process, and customer lifecycle, Interface redesigned everything from materials to take-back programs, becoming a pioneer in closed-loop manufacturing and dramatically reducing its environmental footprint.

Another example is the Ellen MacArthur Foundation, which applies systemic design across industries to promote circularity. Their collaborations with cities like London and companies like H&M show how system mapping, stakeholder engagement, and material innovation can lead to more sustainable urban and industrial ecosystems.

Agriculture

Modern agriculture faces fragmented supply chains, environmental degradation, and unpredictable global markets. Systemic design helps stakeholders—from farmers to retailers—co-create regenerative systems that balance productivity with ecological health.

Example: RegenNetwork applies blockchain and system mapping to create transparent, regenerative agricultural systems. Farmers, scientists, and governments collaborate through shared platforms to monitor, verify, and reward ecological stewardship, creating new market incentives for sustainable practices.

Mobility and Urban Planning

Public transport, urban development, and mobility services increasingly rely on systemic design to create inclusive, efficient, and future-proof solutions.

Example: Mobility-as-a-Service (MaaS) projects, such as Helsinki's Whim app, integrate public transport, car rentals, ride-sharing, and bikes into one seamless interface. By mapping user behaviors, transit infrastructure, and regulatory environments, the system offers personalized and dynamic mobility options while reducing congestion and emissions.

Government and Public Services

Public institutions face systemic fragmentation in policy, service delivery, and citizen engagement. Systemic design offers tools to reframe how governments operate, moving from reactive bureaucracies to proactive, people-centered systems.

Example: MindLab (Denmark) and Policy Lab UK use systemic design to improve public policy.[25] These labs bring together citizens, civil servants, and designers to co-create policies in areas like unemployment, immigration, and digital inclusion, creating solutions that are practical, ethical, and systemically viable.

Governance

One of the best examples of systemic design in organizational governance is the Mondragon Corporation, one of the world's largest federations of worker-owned cooperatives. Founded in the 1950s in a poor, post-war region of Spain, Mondragon reimagined how business, education, finance, and social welfare could be designed to support one another.

Through deeply interconnected systems, Mondragon:

- Links its industrial businesses with cooperative banking (Caja Laboral) to fund growth and resilience.
- Runs its own university (Mondragon University), where education is directly tied to cooperative values and real-world industry needs.
- Shares profits across co-ops, redistributes workers during downturns to prevent layoffs, and gives each member one vote in governance, regardless of role or seniority.

This isn't just a company, it's a self-sustaining ecosystem designed with mutual support and systemic interdependence at its core. Governance is participatory, adaptive, and deeply tied to the values and well-being of its members.

Mondragon shows how economic systems, education, and social equity can be woven into a single, living system—using systemic design not as a methodology, but as an ethos.

Investment

Traditional investment models often focus on short-term returns and isolated KPIs. But systemic investment takes a broader lens—looking at long-term value creation across social, environmental, and economic dimensions. It recognizes that money flows shape systems, and that how and where we invest determines which futures we enable.

Example – The Transform Finance Model:

Transform Finance, a global network and think tank, promotes investment strategies grounded in systems change. They work with impact investors, philanthropic funds, and mission-driven institutions to align capital with social justice and long-term systemic outcomes.

Their framework emphasizes:

- Deep community engagement: Investments are co-designed with the communities they impact.
- Non-extractive finance: Returns are structured to avoid draining value from vulnerable systems.
- Integrated metrics: Success is measured not just in financial growth, but in resilience, equity, and regeneration.

For example, Transform Finance supported investment into worker-owned clean energy cooperatives in the U.S., combining climate action, economic democracy, and racial equity in a single financial model. These investments don't just support one sector—they shift the structural dynamics of ownership, employment, and environmental impact.

Another noteworthy example is Zebras Unite, a cooperative fund and founder community that challenges the unicorn-driven venture capital model. They prioritize regenerative growth, long-term relationships, and ecosystem health over exponential scaling, applying systemic design principles to both how capital is raised and how companies are built.[26]

Systemic investment represents a new frontier in design-driven thinking, where money becomes a tool for redesigning systems, not just fueling them. Systemic Investment enables financing with Interconnected Impact.

There are likely industries and fields emerging right now where systemic design will play a critical role, climate tech, mental health ecosystems, AI ethics, decentralized governance, even space exploration.

Wherever complexity, interdependence, and change collide, systemic design is not just relevant, it's essential.

What's the Problem Behind the Problem?

Birger had a way of making complexity feel approachable, almost playful. He believed that too often, we get stuck solving surface-level problems without looking deeper to uncover the structures and relationships that cause them. His teaching focused on digging into the why, the how, and the connections that shape the system.

His GIGA-mapping exercises—a technique he pioneered—were overwhelming at first, but remarkably satisfying. After extensive research and visualizing, hidden patterns would surface, revealing connections we had never seen before. The GIGA-map became both a revelation and a compass, a tool he used to teach us not to fear the mess, but to embrace it as the birthplace of insight.

Looking back, I sometimes say that systemic design saved me. And I mean that quite literally.

I have ADHD, by the way. I've always been someone who moves through chaos, not by avoiding it, but by constantly trying to make sense of it. My mind doesn't follow a straight line. It jumps, it loops, it dives deep, then zooms out. For a long time, that felt like a flaw. Especially in structured environments where focus, order, and linear thinking are the norm, I felt like I was always too much, too fast, too scattered, too many tabs open.

But building things, starting companies, designing systems, shaping ideas, that's where my brain found its rhythm.

As a founder with ADHD, life often feels like running a hundred processes in parallel. You're thinking about team dynamics, product decisions, investor updates, your own energy levels, the market shifting under your feet, and all of it now. And strangely enough, that's where I found my power. Because systemic design gave me a framework for it. A name for what I was already doing. Tools that helped me take all those non-linear thoughts and visualize them. Make them usable. Shareable. Actionable.

It turned out that my scatteredness wasn't disorder, it was system sensitivity. The ability to hold multiple complex topics in my head, to notice connections others didn't see, to switch contexts without losing the thread, those became my strengths. ADHD didn't go away. It just found a place where it could thrive.

Systemic design didn't just bring order to my chaos, it gave me a language to understand it, a structure to navigate it, and, ultimately, a way to help others turn their own complexity into clarity, agency, and direction.

To close down this chapter, I wanted to say that there are problems behind the problems that the approaches of Mondragon, or Transform Finance address. These deeper problems stem from approximations and myths in economics and business theory, approximations that miss key aspects of the real world. These require incorporating in ways that go beyond cooperatives, employee ownership, or even steward ownership; because the very problem is the design language of owning a business. I will go deeper in this, I promise.

Exercise: Practice Systemic Thinking

Create a System Map for a Real-World Problem
- Pick a complex system you're familiar with, your workplace, your local community, or an industry you're passionate about.
- Identify its key components (stakeholders, processes, resources) and map their relationships.
- Look for leverage points where small changes could create significant impact.

Use an Empathy Map to Understand a Stakeholder
- Choose a specific user or stakeholder within a system you're designing for.
- Complete an empathy map: What do they see, hear, think, feel, say, and do?
- Reflect on how their perspective might influence the design of the system.

Facilitate a Participatory Design Workshop
- Identify a challenge that affects a group of stakeholders.
- Invite a diverse group to co-create solutions using brainstorming, role-playing, or sketching activities.
- Document their feedback and insights, and use them to refine your approach.

Analyze a Fragmented System
- Choose a fragmented system (e.g., healthcare, education, or public transportation).
- Identify the silos and inefficiencies within it.
- Propose a solution based on systemic design principles, focusing on collaboration and communication.

Reflect on Complexity in Your Own Life

- Think about a personal challenge that feels complex or overwhelming.
- Use systemic thinking to map out its components and connections.
- Identify one small change you can make to improve the situation and test its impact.

Embracing complexity is a brave act. Take these assignments as opportunities to explore, experiment, and engage deeply with the systems around you. The insights you uncover might surprise you, and they might just lead to the breakthrough you've been searching for.

In the next chapter, we'll explore how design-driven entrepreneurship builds on these principles to drive innovation and lead to systemic change.

Chapter 6:
Inventing Beyond the Obvious

When we think of innovation, we often picture the "Eureka!" moment — a lone genius having a brilliant idea that "saves the world before breakfast!" But in reality, innovation is rarely about sudden inspiration.

Wait, I'm not contradicting the intro to my book. That spark absolutely exists. But even those moments aren't truly "overnight." They happen after you've sat with complexity long enough to understand it, after you've had the courage to pull apart a messy system, examine its pieces, and reimagine how it could work better. They come when your whole body and soul are breathing and living the challenge.

Innovation, I've come to realize, is less like lightning striking and more like a long, messy, iterative conversation with the world. And design is the language that allows that conversation to happen.

When we think about the great innovations of our time, it's easy to focus on the technology, the microchips, the algorithms, the AI models. But behind every breakthrough is a series of design decisions, choices about how something should work, feel, and fit into people's lives. Design is not just the polish at the end; it's the compass that guides the entire journey. It is as much about the process of discovery as it is about the outcome.

Take Spotify, for example. At its core, Spotify is a technology company, a way to access music files stored on servers. But what made it revolutionary wasn't the streaming technology itself. What set Spotify apart was how its design thinking shaped every decision. From the start, Spotify's team didn't just ask, How do we stream music? They asked, How do we make music feel personal, social, and alive?

That question guided the process. Their designers sat with users, observed how people discovered music, shared mixtapes, or debated songs with friends. They prototyped features, tested them, and iterated quickly. The result? Playlists became a form of self-expression. The "Discover Weekly" feature felt almost magical, as though Spotify understood you better than you understood yourself. The interface was stripped of clutter, keeping the focus on the music rather than the app.[27]

Spotify didn't just deliver music, they designed a new relationship between people and music. And this wasn't accidental. Their innovation process was rooted in design: human-centered research, rapid prototyping, and continuous iteration.

Or consider Oatly, the Swedish oat-milk brand that turned an ordinary product into a global cultural phenomenon. Plant-based milk existed long before Oatly. But Oatly asked a different question: How do we make plant-based milk something people feel proud to drink, not just something they tolerate?

Their team infused design into every stage of development, from product formulation to brand voice. They tested their packaging to feel approachable, fun, and disarmingly honest. Their tone of voice was cheeky and conversational, it didn't just tell you about oat milk, it invited you into a movement. The design process shaped not just how Oatly looked, but how it behaved: its campaigns provoked thought, its copy sparked smiles, and suddenly oat milk wasn't just a dietary swap, it became a statement of identity.[28]

And even in technology-driven sectors, design has been the invisible driver of innovation. Take Figma. They didn't set out to build just another design tool. They started by asking, What if design could be multiplayer? What if collaboration could happen live, in the same file, from anywhere in the world?

Their process was as radical as their product. They observed how teams worked, mapped their pain points, and challenged the assumptions of how design software should work. The decision to make Figma browser-based was not just technical, it was a design choice to remove friction, to democratize access, and to make collaboration effortless.[29]

And as we've mentioned earlier, Airbnb is another example where design shaped not just the result but the process of building trust at scale. In the early days, the founders personally stayed in their hosts' homes, photographed listings themselves, and redesigned the booking flow over and over until it felt safe, simple, and human. The result wasn't just a website; it was a cultural shift. Staying in someone else's home, once considered risky, became an experience people sought out. That leap in trust was a direct outcome of design thinking applied to everything from the interface to the way hosts and guests communicated.[30]

The same is true for Porsche. Yes, Porsche is an engineering powerhouse, but what truly sets it apart is design and legacy, both in product and process, history written on the race track. From their early days at Le Mans, Porsche showed that engineering excellence and perseverance could beat brute force and their GT cars—like the legendary 911 RSR—carry that same spirit of relentless innovation. Porsche has always kept one foot in both worlds: the cutting-edge prototypes that pushed the boundaries of speed and technology, and the GT machines that stayed true to the road-going 911, proving that everyday sports cars could carry racing DNA. That's design in its purest form, not just in the car you drive, but in the philosophy behind it. Precision, elegance, and resilience, distilled into something timeless.[31]

The common thread across all these examples is clear: design guided the journey. It asked better questions, redefined the problem, and shaped solutions that resonated deeply with users. It wasn't just about what these companies built, it was about how they built it.

Over the years, I've had the privilege of working on projects where design was not just the outcome, but the engine of innovation. It forced me to step back, see the bigger picture, and work with people who saw the world completely differently from me.

The Importance of Interdisciplinarity: Blending Design with Business, Technology, and Social Impact

Innovation rarely happens in isolation. The most transformative ideas emerge when different disciplines collide, when a designer thinks like a business strategist, a technologist approaches problems like an artist, and social impact considerations are woven into every decision. This intersection is where design-driven entrepreneurship thrives.

Take business, for instance. Traditional business models often focus on efficiency, scalability, and profitability. But when design enters the equation, the focus shifts to people, how they experience a product, how they interact with a service, and how it fits into their lives. This user-centered perspective ensures that businesses create solutions that resonate on a human level, not just a financial one.

Then there's technology. It gives us the tools to push boundaries, but design teaches us how to use those tools wisely. In the construction world, for instance, digital platforms didn't just make things faster, they reshaped how teams communicate, plan, and collaborate. It wasn't the technology alone that drove progress; it was the design of a system where technology actually solved real, deeply rooted problems.

Social impact is the third essential piece of the puzzle. Without considering the broader implications of our work, innovation risks becoming shortsighted or even harmful. WealthBridge's approach to prefabricated housing is a perfect example of interdisciplinary collaboration. The integration of local labor, cultural context, and sustainable energy wasn't just a design challenge, it was an exercise in blending social impact with business goals and technological innovation.

Interdisciplinarity doesn't just create better solutions, it builds systems that are resilient, adaptable, and scalable. It ensures that design isn't working in isolation but as part of a larger framework that considers the economic, technological, and social ecosystems in which it operates.

In my work, I've seen firsthand how interdisciplinarity sparks innovation. A project might start with a designer sketching an idea, but it evolves when an engineer questions its feasibility, a business strategist calculates its scalability, and a community member asks, "How will this help us?" Each perspective adds a layer of depth, transforming good ideas into great ones.

For design-driven entrepreneurs, the lesson is clear: embrace the intersections. Seek out collaborators who think differently, ask questions that challenge assumptions, and build solutions that blend the best of every discipline. The future of innovation depends on it.

Exercise

1. Rapid Experiment Challenge
 In one hour:
- Pick a small design problem (e.g., "How might I make mornings less stressful?").
- Sketch three radically different solutions.
- Choose one, make a quick prototype (paper mockup, storyboard, or clickable draft).
- Test it with one person and ask: "How does this feel?"
- Reflect: What did you learn about the process of designing, not just the outcome?

2. The Conversation with the World
Write a journal entry starting with:
"If innovation is a conversation with the world, what question am I asking right now?" Reflect on how you're listening, to users, to collaborators, to emerging patterns, and what responses you're getting back.

3. Capstone: The Design Compass Project
Design your own "Innovation Compass" — a one-page visual that shows:
- The principles that guide your creative process
- The questions you ask before you build
- The checkpoints that keep your work human-centered

You can use metaphors (journey, ecosystem, circuit board) or create a literal compass. Present it as your personal design manifesto.

Whether you're redesigning a single product or rethinking an entire industry, design opens doors to innovation you never thought possible. Now it's your turn to dive in, experiment, and create. Start small, think big, and trust the process— because the industries of tomorrow are shaped by people like you.

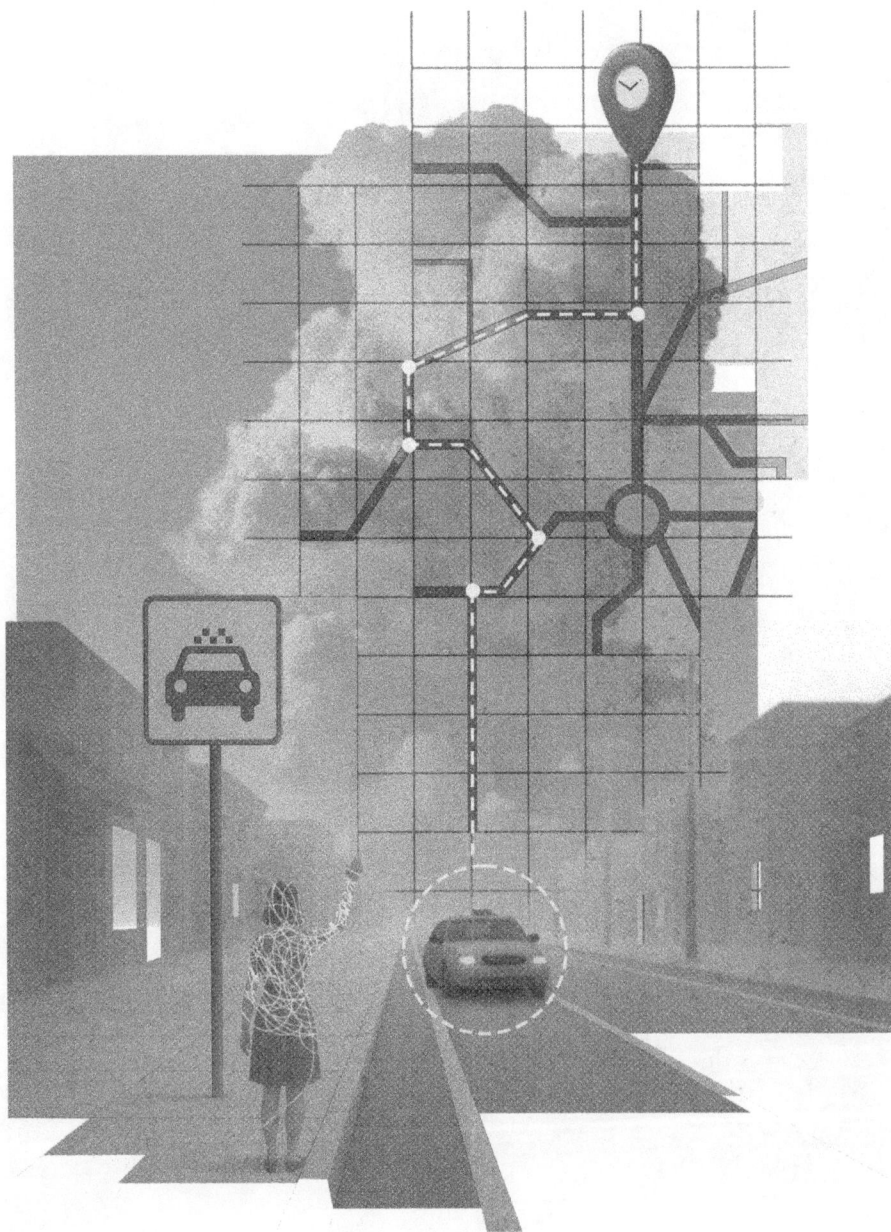

Chapter 7:
Building from Scratch – A Way Of Life

Building from scratch isn't just something entrepreneurs do at work, for many of them, it's who they are. It's in the way they think, the way they live, the way they approach even the smallest challenges. And for me, it became clear early on that some people simply cannot help but build, no matter the circumstances.

In my family entrepreneurship was the air everyone breathed. Industry, social impact, and the act of building something meaningful weren't abstract concepts; they were lived, day in and day out. Our family dinners were never quiet. They were filled with debate, brainstorming, and dreaming. People would talk about problems they saw in their businesses, in their communities, in the world, and then discuss how to solve them. Looking back, I realize those conversations were training for everything I do today. They taught me that ideas are currency, that action is non-negotiable, and that building is something you do even when everything around you is falling apart.

So when I talk about "building from scratch," it isn't a metaphor. I have seen businesses collapse and be rebuilt. I have watched people lose everything and still wake up the next day ready to try again. I grew up in an environment where creating wasn't optional, it was survival. And when people grow up like that, starting over isn't frightening. It is simply the next step.

This is why so many entrepreneurs who build something from scratch aren't just doing a job. They are living out who they are. Building, iterating, and reinventing isn't work for them, it's identity. It's waking up in the middle of the night with a new idea, sketching solutions on napkins, staying up late not because they have to, but because they can't stop.

The world tends to celebrate finished products: the sleek iPhone, the global empire of Starbucks, the seamless magic of Netflix. But the early days of these ventures were anything but polished.

Apple started with two guys in a garage, hand-assembling circuit boards and pitching them to a local computer store.

Starbucks wasn't always a café, its first iteration just sold coffee beans and equipment.

Netflix mailed DVDs in red envelopes long before streaming became its defining move.

Each of these companies began not with certainty, but with an unanswered question: What if?

- What if personal computers were beautiful and intuitive, not clunky and intimidating? (Apple)
- What if high-quality coffee wasn't just a luxury for Italians but a ritual for Americans too? (Starbucks)
- What if people could have access to thousands of movies without late fees or driving to Blockbuster? (Netflix)

The founders didn't have roadmaps, they had courage. They built not just companies, but entire categories where none existed.

And building from scratch is messy. It's about wrestling with the unknown:

- Convincing suppliers to trust you when you have no track record.
- Persuading talented people to leave safer jobs to join your idea.
- Explaining a concept to investors who raise their eyebrows and say, "But does anyone even want this?"

Take Sara Blakely, founder of Spanx. She didn't just create a product, she created a category that didn't exist. With $5,000 in savings, she cold-called factories until one agreed to take a chance on her. She wrote her own patent. She convinced Neiman Marcus to carry her product by literally changing into it mid-meeting in the bathroom to show its power. That's building from scratch: turning rejection into fuel and persistence into progress.[32]

Or consider Airbnb's early days (again!). The founders couldn't get funding, investors didn't believe people would let strangers sleep in their homes. So they maxed out credit cards, designed their own cereal boxes to raise cash ("Obama O's" and "Cap'n McCain's"), and spent months living with their first customers to understand exactly what was broken about the travel industry. Airbnb didn't just design a website; they designed trust into a completely new market.[33]

Building something unheard-of is never linear. You're constantly iterating, often throwing out what you built yesterday because you've learned something new today. It takes grit to keep going when you feel like you're starting over again and again. But that's also the beauty of it, every "restart" makes the venture sharper, more resilient, more aligned with the people it is meant to serve.

And this process is not just about solving problems, it's about becoming the kind of person who can hold space for uncertainty and still move forward. Building from scratch requires you to be visionary and pragmatic, dreamer and doer, artist and accountant, all in one.

Perhaps the hardest part is that no one will ever believe in your idea as much as you do in the beginning. That belief has to be yours to carry, through the sleepless nights, the pivots, the rejections, the "what if I fail?" moments. And when you finally see someone using what you created, loving it, sharing it, that's when the world begins to catch up with the vision you've been holding alone for so long.

The Myth of Work–Life Balance

Whenever I'm invited to speak at conferences, one question almost always comes up:

"How do you manage work–life balance?"

And my honest answer is always the same: *I don't believe in it.*

Not because I don't value rest, family, or well-being, I do. But the very idea of "balance" suggests that work and life are two separate entities sitting on opposite sides of a scale, constantly competing for attention. For entrepreneurs, especially those who build from scratch, this distinction feels artificial. When your work is an expression of who you are, there's no clean line between the office and your living room, between your calendar and your heartbeat.

The notion of "work–life balance" is actually a relatively new invention. Before the Industrial Revolution, work and life were deeply intertwined. Farmers, artisans, and merchants worked where they lived, often alongside family members. Work was not something you "went to" — it was part of the rhythm of existence, inseparable from community and culture. It was the rise of the factory system in the 18th and 19th centuries that introduced the idea of clocking in and clocking out, creating a strict divide between "work time" and "personal time."

This system, efficient but dehumanizing, became what I call modern productivity traps. Humans became parts of a larger machine, measured by their output per hour. Eventually, work–life balance emerged as a coping mechanism: a way for workers to reclaim some semblance of life outside the grind. It was an important social advance, but it also cemented the idea that work and life were at odds, something to be balanced rather than integrated.

But when you are building from scratch, you are no longer a cog, you are the one designing the machine. And that changes everything.

I've been asked whether this means I "live to work." The answer is no, I work to live in the truest sense of the phrase, because the work I do is a reflection of my life's values, my family's legacy, and the ideas I care about most. I don't turn that off at 5 p.m. any more than I turn off being a daughter, a friend, or a human being.

Some of the most transformative ideas I've ever had didn't come while sitting in a meeting room, they came during conversations with friends over dinner, while traveling between countries, or walking by the ocean. Design and entrepreneurship don't punch a timecard; they're living, breathing processes that keep evolving even when you're not "at work."

Consider founders like Yvon Chouinard of Patagonia, who built a company that reflected his personal ethos of environmental stewardship, his work was his activism, his lifestyle, his identity.[34] Or Elon Musk, whose multiple ventures seem less like separate companies and more like extensions of one singular obsession: accelerating humanity's future. For people like this, the question isn't "how do you balance work and life?" but "how do you design a life where your work is worth living for?"

Even outside entrepreneurship, some of the world's most impactful figures have treated their life's work as inseparable from their life. Maya Angelou didn't write between the hours of nine and five, her writing was the lens through which she processed existence. Walt Disney didn't clock out of imagination at the end of the day, he lived inside it.

The problem with the work–life balance narrative is that it often sets people up for guilt on both sides: guilt for working too much, or guilt for not working enough. But for those who build from scratch, work is not a distraction from life, it's a contribution to it. It's the way you bring your values, your ideas, and your vision into the world.

Of course, this doesn't mean glorifying burnout or ignoring rest. The difference is that rest becomes part of the work itself, a time for creative incubation, reflection, and renewal, not an escape from it. When I take time off, I don't "stop thinking about work." I stop forcing it and allow inspiration to find me again, in the quiet moments where clarity often hides.

So when people ask me about work–life balance, I tell them this:

Stop trying to split yourself in two. Instead, integrate. Design a life where the work you do is an authentic extension of who you are, where your values are present in your projects, where your creativity spills over into your evenings, and where your mornings are filled with purpose.

Because for those of us who build from scratch, there is no switch to flip on or off. There is just a life, and we spend it building.

Making Money vs Getting Money

I still remember the first time I made my own money. I was 14, shy but secretly proud of the one thing that set me apart, my style and intonations in English. It wasn't just good; it was confident, with a natural fluency that sounded different from what most people had been taught in school. That was my selling edge.

Adults — people much older than me — would come to our home for private lessons. They were preparing for embassy interviews, IELTS exams, visa appointments, and they needed someone who could help them practice. That someone turned out to be me.

It was a strange feeling at first, sitting across from grown-ups and correcting their sentences, asking them to repeat after me, and watching them take notes as if every word I said mattered. And then, at the end of each week, came the envelope of cash. That moment changed me forever. I wasn't just receiving money, I was making it. I had created value, solved a problem, and been paid for it. That realization was electrifying.

Looking back, I think that was the first time I understood what entrepreneurship truly is. It's not about waiting for someone to hand you something. It's about creating something that didn't exist before and letting it earn its place in the world. There's a big difference between making money and getting money. Making money means you've built something valuable enough that people willingly exchange their resources for it. Getting money is just a transfer — a grant, a loan, an investment — not yet tied to proof that your idea really works.

I see so many founders fall into the trap of chasing money rather than making it. It's seductive, because raising funds feels like validation. A term sheet, a bank transfer, a headline on TechCrunch, it can feel like you've made it. But I've seen too many startups burn through their capital without ever finding product-market fit. I've seen teams grow too fast, hire too soon, and spend their energy managing complexity they didn't need yet. They were chasing the illusion of success instead of creating real value.

When I was teaching "how to look native in English" at 14, no one gave me money because they liked me or wanted to "support young entrepreneurs." They paid because they were nervous about their embassy interviews and needed someone to help them prepare. The money was proof that I had made their lives better. That's the discipline of making money, it's not glamorous, but it's deeply satisfying.

History is full of entrepreneurs who understood this instinctively. I mentioned Sara Blakely before. She started Spanx with $5,000 of her own savings and sold her first batches of shapewear by going store to store, explaining why her product mattered. She didn't raise money until she had proof that women wanted what she was making. Also going back to Yvon Chouinard, founder of Patagonia, he started by forging climbing gear for himself and his friends, selling it out of his car before building a global company that now leads in environmental activism. Mailchimp, one of the world's most successful email marketing platforms, never raised venture funding — they grew entirely from customer revenue, slowly and steadily, until they were acquired for $12 billion.[35]

Contrast this with companies like Juicero[36] or Quibi, which raised hundreds of millions before truly validating their business models. Juicero built a $400 juice machine that no one needed, and Quibi poured nearly $2 billion into short-form video content before learning that consumers didn't want to watch premium TV shows in 10-minute chunks.[37] Even WeWork, with its charismatic founder and billions in capital, collapsed spectacularly because the business model was not as scalable or profitable as investors wanted to believe. These are cautionary tales of what happens when founders and investors focus on raising money instead of making money, the burn rate goes up, expectations soar, and the company becomes a runaway train headed off the tracks.

Investors share responsibility for this trap. Early-stage investors often pressure founders to grow faster than is healthy, to optimize for valuation rather than validation.

And then there are those with a bit of money to spare who like to call themselves "business angels." They may mean well, and perhaps genuinely believe they're helping, but too often they end up wasting founders' most precious resource: time. Their endless requests for more documents, more calls, and more "refinements" that lead nowhere, all while founders are pulled away from building their product and talking to their customers. Unfortunately, this behavior ends up diluting the very meaning of "business angel," overshadowing the truly committed early-stage investors who take real risks, offer hands-on guidance, and open doors that change a startup's trajectory.

The worst part is that this process can convince founders that fundraising is the work, when in reality it should only ever be fuel for the work. This dynamic can damage founders' confidence and distort their priorities. Instead of refining their offering and earning their first revenue, they get stuck in a cycle of trying to impress investors. It's like building a house for the bank's approval rather than the people who will live in it. The healthiest founder-investor relationships are the ones where both sides are aligned on creating real value first, and only then scaling it with capital.

Throughout history, businesses have survived by making money, not just getting it. Farmers sold their crops to buy seed for the next season. Artisans sold what they crafted so they could keep working. It was simple and direct. It wasn't until the industrial era that we started building companies with other people's money upfront, financing railways, factories, and big infrastructure. And in the last decade, with cheap capital everywhere, we've pushed that even further, raising money first, hoping to figure out the rest later.

But there's something grounding about making money first. It forces you to get close to your customers, to design something they truly want, to listen to them and adapt. It teaches you discipline. When you make your own money, you spend it differently. You protect it. You respect it.

This doesn't mean raising money is bad, it can be powerful fuel when used at the right time. But it should accelerate something that already works, not replace the hard work of figuring it out. The best companies, from IKEA to Amazon, were obsessed with their customers long before they were obsessed with their investors. They designed their businesses to generate cash flow, to prove value every step of the way, and only then did they use capital to grow.

For me, that first experience of earning money wasn't just about financial independence, it was about my identity as an entrepreneur.

Turning a Dream into a Scalable Enterprise: Building Systems and Empowering Others to Lead

Scaling a business is one of the most misunderstood and underestimated challenges in entrepreneurship. Starting a company is hard, yes, but in many ways, it's a different game entirely. In the early days, you can run on adrenaline and improvisation, patching leaks as they appear, making decisions on instinct, personally touching every part of the process. But growth is unforgiving. It magnifies weaknesses, exposes inefficiencies, and tests whether your dream was built on sand or stone. Scaling is less about working harder and more about working differently. It means building structures that allow your business to grow without falling apart, and that requires an entirely new skill set.

We've all seen companies stumble at this stage. WeWork is one of the most striking examples. At its peak, it was valued at $47 billion, celebrated as the future of work. But beneath the glossy branding and charismatic founder narrative, processes were chaotic, financial discipline was weak, and governance was shaky. When WeWork tried to go public, all of this became glaringly obvious. The dream unraveled, not because there wasn't demand for flexible workspaces, but because the company's systems couldn't support its scale.[38]

Contrast that with Shopify, which faced its own critical moment as e-commerce exploded. Shopify started as a small online snowboard shop, then pivoted to empower other merchants. Scaling wasn't just a matter of acquiring more users;

they had to build a platform robust enough to support millions of businesses across the globe. They invested heavily in developer tools, logistics, and payments infrastructure so that Shopify could grow without breaking under its own weight. The difference wasn't just vision, it was discipline and foresight.

Another example is Slack, whose rapid growth could have easily fractured the company. Instead, they scaled deliberately, building internal documentation, customer support systems, and product roadmaps that preserved user experience even as their user base ballooned. They treated scaling as a design challenge, creating processes and rituals to maintain quality at speed.

And then there are cautionary tales like Quibi, the short-form streaming platform that raised nearly $2 billion but shut down within six months. Quibi's failure wasn't due to lack of funding or talent but because they tried to scale a product that hadn't yet proven product–market fit. They poured resources into star-studded content and splashy marketing campaigns before confirming whether users wanted what they were offering. Scaling too fast magnified the flaws in the model and left no room to course-correct.

I experienced the highs and lows of scaling firsthand with ENFA – the Euro-Nordic Funding Alliance. When I founded ENFA, I had a simple but ambitious vision: build a systemic, scalable model for international collaboration that could deliver measurable impact. What began as a concept became, in just two years, a network spanning 20 countries — innovators, investors, institutions, and governments collaborating to accelerate social, economic, and technological transformation.

But the journey wasn't smooth. Building ENFA meant building trust — over and over again, in country after country. I spent two years traveling, meeting people face-to-face, listening, and carefully handpicking partners with proven expertise and deep networks. Many times, I heard "no" before I heard "yes." There were moments when I questioned whether it was possible to align so many players across so many borders.

What made ENFA grow wasn't just systems or strategy, it was relationships. I didn't just offer partners membership; I offered them ownership in the mission.

Each partner became a representative of ENFA in their country, responsible for opening doors, building local ecosystems, and shaping the network's future. This shared-ownership model became ENFA's backbone. It allowed us to scale rapidly while staying grounded in trust, collaboration, and aligned incentives.

Today, ENFA connects organizations into high-value, cross-border consortia, blends public and private financing, and gives its members tailored guidance and strategic visibility. But behind the scenes, ENFA is a lesson in what scaling really requires: designing a system that grows stronger with each new connection rather than weaker under the weight of growth.

This is what companies like IKEA have done so well. Their flat-pack furniture wasn't just a clever design, it was a logistics breakthrough that allowed them to scale globally without prohibitive shipping costs. Toyota, too, understood that scaling wasn't just about producing more cars but producing them with consistent quality. By empowering every worker to stop the production line if they spotted a flaw, Toyota scaled excellence, not just output.

And here's where systemic design comes in. Scaling isn't just about adding more, it's about looking at your venture as a living system. Systemic design invites you to map every actor, every process, every point of friction, and redesign them so that growth creates harmony rather than chaos. It's the difference between a messy tangle of wires that somehow works — until you add one more — and a well-laid circuit board where every new connection makes the system stronger. When you approach scaling through a systemic design lens, you stop patching problems reactively and start engineering resilience.

For me, this has meant treating every scaling effort as an iterative experiment: mapping our processes, spotting bottlenecks, inviting partners into co-creation sessions, and constantly asking whether our growth was aligned with our mission. It meant knowing when to standardize and when to stay flexible, when to automate and when to keep human judgment in the loop.

The pattern is clear: companies that succeed at scaling treat it as a design problem. They create systems that are repeatable yet flexible, robust yet adaptable. They find the balance between structure and creativity.

When done well, scaling transforms your venture into something that no longer relies on you being everywhere at once. It becomes an organism capable of growing, adapting, and making an impact long after you've stepped out of the room.

Exercis: The Modern Builder's Edition

Each exercise invites you to think like a designer, act like a strategist, and lead like a founder who's building for both purpose and growth.

1. Anchor in the Problem, Not the Product

Goal: Ensure your venture grows from genuine insight, not assumption.

Steps:

- Write down the core problem you want to solve, in one sentence.
- Now describe who experiences it most acutely.
- Conduct three short conversations with people who live that problem daily.
- After each, refine your problem statement, make it sharper, smaller, and more human.

Reflection:

How did your understanding change after listening?

If your product disappeared tomorrow, would the problem still matter deeply to you?

2. Create a Value Flow Map

Goal: Visualize how value moves through your ecosystem, and where it gets stuck.

Steps:

- Choose one industry or challenge area.
- Map out every key actor (customers, partners, suppliers, regulators, communities).
- Draw arrows showing who gives and who receives value, money, time, trust, or attention.
- Identify one bottleneck or blind spot where value leaks or tension builds.
- Outcome:

A single-page diagram that helps you see where small changes could shift the entire system.

3. The One-Day Prototype

Goal: Turn an idea into something visible — fast.

Steps:

- Choose one problem area from your Value Flow Map.
- Sketch or storyboard one possible solution.
- In a single day, make a basic prototype: a visual mockup, landing page, or short explainer video.
- Share it with five people who resemble your intended audience.
- Ask only two questions:

    "What part of this feels useful?"

    "What part feels confusing or unnecessary?"

Reflection:

What did you learn that no amount of planning could have revealed?

4. Design a Repeatable Process

Goal: Build systems that scale your time and reduce chaos.

Steps:

- Pick one activity you repeat often (like onboarding, sales outreach, or reporting).
- Write down every step in plain language.
- Mark which steps are:

    Repeatable

    Automatable

    Delegatable

- Simplify or automate one of them this week.

Outcome:

You'll create a clear, teachable process that grows with your team instead of draining your energy.

Chapter 8:
The Real Help Entrepreneurs Need

It was a sunny afternoon when I found myself sitting across from a bright-eyed entrepreneur at a startup accelerator event. He was animated, talking about his vision for a sustainable packaging solution that could revolutionize the industry. His pitch was polished, his prototype promising, and yet, there was something in his tone, a quiet edge of exhaustion.

"I've been pitching to investors non-stop for months," he admitted when I asked about his journey so far. "The feedback is always the same: 'Great idea, but come back when you're further along.' How am I supposed to get further along when all my time is spent chasing funding?"

It wasn't the first time I'd heard this story. As I looked around the room, I realized how many of the founders here were caught in the same cycle, brilliant ideas, endless pitches, and an overwhelming sense of isolation. Despite all the resources offered by incubators, accelerators, and venture capitalists, something was missing.

That moment stayed with me. It was clear that the current support systems for entrepreneurs, while helpful in some ways, weren't designed to address the full scope of challenges founders face. They provided funding, mentorship, and networking opportunities, but they rarely addressed the systemic pressures that weigh entrepreneurs down, the operational chaos, the lack of mental and emotional support, or the pressure to scale at all costs.

I started wondering: What if we could rethink these support models? What if we could create spaces that didn't just hand founders tools but actually worked alongside them to design better systems? What if we focused not just on growth but on sustainability, innovation, and impact?

This chapter explores that vision. It examines the strengths and shortcomings of traditional models like incubators, accelerators, and venture capital, and introduces new, design-driven approaches, venture studios, rich design spaces, and Business hubs, that prioritize collaboration, creativity, and long-term success. Because supporting entrepreneurs isn't just about funding their ideas, it's about designing ecosystems where their ideas can thrive.

The Valley of Death: Where Startups are Truly Tested

If starting a business is like planting a seed, and scaling is like tending a tree, then the valley of death is the barren stretch of land you must cross between those two points, the place where most startups perish.

The valley of death refers to that treacherous stage after the initial excitement of a launch, but before a company becomes financially sustainable. It's when costs are high, revenues are low (or non-existent), and every decision feels existential. Investors often call this "runway," founders call it "survival mode," and anyone who's been there knows that this is where grit, creativity, and systems-thinking matter most.

When I first learned about the valley of death, it was described as a graph, a curve that dips below zero before climbing again. But the reality is far messier. It's late-night phone calls with your co-founder wondering if you can make payroll.

It's pitching your idea over and over, only to hear polite rejections. It's asking yourself if you're crazy to keep going.

This isn't unique to early-stage founders, the graveyard of business history is full of examples of companies that didn't survive their valley of death.

Take Segway, the hyped-up "revolution in personal transportation." When it launched in 2001, it had backing from tech luminaries like Steve Jobs and Jeff Bezos, but it never crossed the adoption chasm. The product was expensive, city infrastructure wasn't ready, and regulatory hurdles made it impractical. Segway burned through capital without ever reaching mass-market viability, eventually selling to a Chinese robotics company and ending production in 2020.

Or consider Jawbone, once a darling of Silicon Valley for its sleek Bluetooth headsets and fitness trackers. Jawbone raised nearly a billion dollars in venture funding but spent too much too fast on marketing and inventory, while rivals like Fitbit iterated quickly and grabbed market share. Jawbone couldn't survive its valley, its costs outran its revenue, and it shut down in 2017.

On the flip side, there are companies that navigated the valley with painful discipline and came out stronger. Amazon is one of the most famous examples, it spent years operating at a loss, reinvesting every cent into growth, logistics, and infrastructure.

Many analysts predicted its collapse in the early 2000s, but Jeff Bezos kept the company focused on long-term strategy rather than short-term profits. Today, Amazon is synonymous with resilience through the valley of death.

Another example is Netflix, which almost didn't survive its transition from DVD rentals to streaming. When they pivoted, they faced skyrocketing content costs, a skeptical market, and a nearly disastrous attempt to split their DVD business into a separate brand (remember Qwikster?). But by learning from missteps, renegotiating deals, and focusing relentlessly on streaming, they not only survived, they reshaped an entire industry.

What these examples show is that the valley of death isn't just about money. It's about clarity, adaptability, and emotional stamina. You need to know what problem you're solving, who you're solving it for, and be willing to test, fail, and adjust until you find traction. You also need to build trust, with your team, your customers, and your investors, because without that, there is no bridge across the valley.

From my own ventures, I've seen how crucial it is to design for survival early on. This doesn't mean being risk-averse, it means being intentional. It means mapping out where your biggest vulnerabilities are: cash flow, team capacity, customer acquisition, and addressing them proactively.

It means building lightweight systems that let you pivot quickly without losing coherence. And it means maintaining a relentless focus on why you started in the first place, because in the valley, your "why" is often the only thing that keeps you going.

In systemic design terms, the valley of death is where your idea is stress-tested against reality. It's where weak assumptions are exposed and where founders must decide whether to double down, pivot, or walk away. Systemic design tools like GIGA-mapping or journey mapping can be lifesavers here, helping you see not just the surface-level problem but the root causes, and uncovering leverage points where small changes can create big impact.

Analyzing Current Support Mechanisms: Incubators, Accelerators, and Venture Capital

The startup ecosystem is teeming with support mechanisms, each offering unique advantages for entrepreneurs. Incubators, accelerators, and venture capital firms have long been pillars of this ecosystem, providing funding, mentorship, and networks to help startups succeed. However, as I've observed through years of working with entrepreneurs, these models, while valuable, often fail to address the deeper, systemic challenges that founders face.

Incubators: A Nurturing Start, But Limited Momentum

Incubators are designed to provide early-stage startups with resources like office space, mentorship, and access to networks. They aim to nurture ideas from their earliest stages, often focusing on building strong foundations for business models and prototypes. However, this model tends to lack urgency.

Many entrepreneurs I've spoken with describe incubators as safe, even comfortable, but not particularly transformative. Without clear timelines or goals, startups can linger too long in the development phase, delaying their market entry and missing critical opportunities. While incubators excel at creating a nurturing environment, they sometimes fail to push founders toward the next big step.

Accelerators: Speed Meets Pressure

Accelerators take a different approach. These intensive programs, typically lasting three to six months, are designed to fast-track startups with a minimum viable product (MVP). In exchange for equity, accelerators provide seed funding, mentorship, and a powerful network of investors and peers.

The success stories are impressive, programs like Y Combinator have launched companies worth billions. However, this fast-paced model isn't for everyone. I've seen founders struggle with compressed timelines, especially when their ideas require longer development cycles. Accelerators can also create an intense focus on scaling quickly, which sometimes leads to shortcuts or compromises in building a sustainable foundation.

Venture Capital: Fueling Growth, But at a Cost

Venture capital is often seen as the ultimate milestone for startups. With substantial funding, startups can expand rapidly, hire top talent, and dominate their markets. But this model comes with strings attached. Venture capital firms typically demand significant equity and a degree of control, pushing startups to prioritize rapid growth and high returns.

For some businesses, this works brilliantly. But for others, especially those focused on systemic change or long-term impact, the pressure to scale at all costs can be detrimental. I've seen founders pivot away from their original vision simply to meet the expectations of their investors, losing the heart of what made their venture meaningful in the first place.

Where These Models Fall Short

- Through my work, I've come to realize that traditional support mechanisms often focus on addressing surface-level needs: funding, mentorship, and networking. While these are important, they don't address the deeper, systemic pressures that weigh on founders:

- Operational Overload: Founders are often expected to handle everything, from strategy to day-to-day tasks, leaving little room for creativity or long-term planning.

- Lack of Holistic Support: Traditional models rarely account for the mental and emotional toll of entrepreneurship or provide systems to manage it.

- One-Size-Fits-All Approaches: Many support programs impose rigid timelines or metrics, failing to adapt to the unique needs of each venture.

These limitations are why so many entrepreneurs feel burnt out, isolated, or stuck in a cycle of pitching and fundraising without making meaningful progress.

The Need for a Rethink

This is where design-driven entrepreneurship (DDE) comes in. Traditional models, while valuable, often focus on outputs, funding secured, valuations raised, without considering the systems that drive sustainable success. By contrast, DDE-inspired models like venture studios, rich design spaces, and Business hubs focus on creating ecosystems where founders can thrive, balancing short-term goals with long-term impact.

In the next section, we'll explore how these alternative models address the gaps in traditional support systems, providing founders with the tools, resources, and environments they need to succeed, not just in scaling their ventures, but in designing meaningful solutions for the challenges they care about.

Introducing DDE-Inspired Models

In the evolving landscape of entrepreneurship, traditional support mechanisms like incubators, accelerators, and venture capital (VC) firms have been instrumental in nurturing startups. However, as the entrepreneurial ecosystem matures, new models inspired by Design-Driven Entrepreneurship (DDE) are emerging, offering more integrated and holistic support structures. Among these are venture studios, rich design spaces, and business hubs, each addressing existing challenges and fostering better outcomes for both founders and investors.

Venture Studios: A Comprehensive Approach to Startup Creation

Venture studios, also known as startup studios, represent a paradigm shift in how startups are conceived and developed. Unlike traditional models that primarily offer mentorship or funding, venture studios actively participate in the creation of startups from the ground up. They generate ideas internally, validate them, and then build companies by providing resources, expertise, and capital.

This model offers several advantages:

- Increased Success Rates: Startups emerging from venture studios often exhibit higher success rates compared to those from traditional accelerators or incubators. For instance, venture studio startups have a 30% higher success rate than traditional startups.
- Resource Efficiency: By centralizing resources such as legal, marketing, and technical support, venture studios enable startups to operate more efficiently, allowing founders to focus on core product development and market strategies.
- Rapid Market Entry: The collaborative environment within a venture studio accelerates the development process, facilitating quicker validation and market entry.

A notable example is High Alpha Innovation, which combines venture funding with a studio model to systematically launch and scale startups. Their approach has led to the successful creation of multiple high-growth companies.

Rich Design Spaces: Fostering Creativity and Innovation

Rich design spaces are environments specifically crafted to stimulate creativity, collaboration, and innovative thinking. These spaces are equipped with tools, technologies, and resources that encourage experimentation and rapid prototyping.

Key features include:

- Collaborative Environments: By bringing together individuals from diverse disciplines, rich design spaces foster cross-pollination of ideas, leading to innovative solutions.
- Access to Advanced Tools: These spaces provide access to cutting-edge technologies and prototyping tools, enabling entrepreneurs to quickly bring their ideas to life.
- Mentorship and Guidance: Experienced mentors are often available to provide insights and guidance, helping to navigate complex design and development challenges.

While specific statistical data on rich design spaces is limited, their qualitative impact on fostering innovation and supporting early-stage development is widely recognized in the entrepreneurial community.

Business Hubs: Integrating Ecosystems for Sustainable Growth

Business hubs take a holistic approach to entrepreneurship by integrating various stakeholders within an ecosystem, including startups, corporations, investors, academia, and government entities. These hubs aim to create a synergistic environment where resources, knowledge, and opportunities are shared to promote sustainable growth.

Benefits of business hubs include:

- Resource Sharing: Pooling resources among participants reduces costs and increases access to necessary tools and services.
- Enhanced Networking: Facilitated interactions among diverse stakeholders lead to partnerships, collaborations, and new business opportunities.
- Sustainable Development: By focusing on systemic integration, these hubs promote long-term sustainability over short-term gains.

Station F in Paris exemplifies a business hub. As the world's largest startup campus, it houses over 1,000 startups and offers more than 30 programs, creating a comprehensive ecosystem for innovation.[39]

Addressing Challenges and Creating Better Outcomes

These DDE-inspired models address several limitations inherent in traditional support mechanisms:

- Holistic Support: By providing comprehensive resources and active involvement, they mitigate the operational overload often experienced by founders.
- Tailored Development: The flexibility inherent in these models allows for customized support, accommodating the unique needs and timelines of different startups.
- Sustainable Growth: Emphasizing systemic integration and long-term planning reduces the pressure for rapid scaling, promoting sustainable business practices.

For investors, these models offer diversified portfolios with potentially higher success rates due to the structured and hands-on approach to company building. Founders benefit from a supportive ecosystem that not only provides capital but also strategic guidance, resources, and mentorship, significantly enhancing the likelihood of success.

In the end, venture studios, rich design spaces, and Business hubs represent a progressive evolution in entrepreneurial support. By embracing these models, the startup ecosystem can overcome existing challenges, leading to more successful and sustainable ventures that benefit both founders and investors alike.

It's Not a Fully New Thing, It's an Iteration

This isn't just a shift in how we support startups, it's a redesign of what success looks like. It's no longer about chasing the next round of funding or scaling at breakneck speed. It's about creating resilient, impactful businesses that solve real problems and leave a lasting legacy.m

But it's only fair for you, as an entrepreneur reading this book to have the chance to assess your support system. So, here are some exercises to help you do just that.

Exercises: Assess Your Resources

Audit Your Current Support System
Take stock of the resources, networks, and support mechanisms you currently rely on.
- Who's in Your Corner? List the people, programs, or organizations supporting your venture (e.g., mentors, accelerators, VCs).
- What's Working? Identify the aspects of your support system that are helping you succeed.
- What's Missing? Pinpoint gaps, such as a lack of operational support, creativity tools, or emotional guidance.

Goal: Gain a clear understanding of where you're thriving and where you need more help to align your support system with your goals.

Design Your Ideal Venture Studio
Imagine creating your own venture studio designed to help entrepreneurs like yourself.
- Core Services: What operational, financial, and strategic support would it provide?
- Creative Processes: How would it foster innovation, from ideation to prototyping?
- Team Dynamics: Who would you bring in to mentor, guide, or collaborate with entrepreneurs?

Goal: Visualize how a centralized support system could transform the way you build and scale your venture.

3. Prototype a Rich Design Space for Your Startup
If you could design a space to bring your ideas to life, what would it look like?
- Tools You'd Need: List the resources that would accelerate your development (e.g., prototyping tools, brainstorming spaces).
- Your Collaboration Network: Who would you invite to work alongside you in

this space? Think of experts, peers, and mentors.

- A Real Problem to Solve: Focus on one challenge your startup is facing and outline how you'd address it in this space.

Goal: Develop a plan for leveraging collaborative, creative environments to move your venture forward.

4. Identify Your Business hub

Think about how you can create an ecosystem that connects your venture to larger networks.

- Who Would Be Involved? List potential collaborators, such as corporate partners, other startups, policymakers, or academic institutions.
- Shared Goals: Identify a challenge or opportunity that this ecosystem could address collectively.
- Steps to Engage: Outline how you could start building these relationships, whether through networking, partnerships, or shared initiatives.

Goal: Position your startup within a larger system where collaboration and resource-sharing amplify your impact.

5. Set Metrics for Success

Define success for your venture and the ecosystem around it.

- What Matters to You? List the key metrics that align with your mission (e.g., user satisfaction, social impact, revenue growth).
- How Will You Measure Them? Identify tools or systems for tracking your progress.
- How Will You Act on Insights? Create a plan for using this data to refine your strategies and ensure alignment with your goals.

Goal: Keep your startup focused on long-term impact, ensuring that growth aligns with your values.

Final Challenge: Redesign Your Support Model

Take everything you've learned in this chapter and reimagine your support system.

- Combine elements of venture studios, rich design spaces, and búsiness hubs.
- Think about how these changes could address your current challenges and amplify your strengths.
- Share your ideas with a mentor, advisor, or peer to get feedback and refine your plan.

Goal: Build a support system that empowers you to focus on innovation, sustainability, and impact while providing the tools and resources you need to thrive.

You don't have to accept support systems as they are—you can design ones that work for you. By rethinking your approach and embracing models that prioritize collaboration, creativity, and long-term success, you can build a foundation that supports not just your venture, but your vision for the future. Now it's time to start designing the system that will help you thrive.

Chapter 9:
Design in the "Wilderness"[1]

I sometimes joke that I brought the so-called refugee crisis to Europe in 2015, the same year I landed in Oslo to begin my master's studies in design. It was a light-hearted way to describe a heavy transition, but what followed that year changed the course of my life and career entirely.

Not long after I arrived, I found myself volunteering on the Greek islands, where waves of displaced people were arriving daily. I helped with translation and basic aid, working face-to-face with individuals who were navigating a reality far more complex than I had ever experienced. Around that same time, our school introduced a course called Design in Transit, a timely intersection of education and real-world need.

---

1   Inspired by Brené Brown's 2017 book: Braving the Wilderness: The Quest for True Belonging and the Courage to Stand Alone.

We became design students who went beyond theory and entered the field, working inside refugee reception centers to design for and with people in transition.

That's when At Home in Transition was born, what began as a project evolved into a lifelong pursuit.

While working in these highly transient environments, I found myself repeatedly asking a simple but deep question: How do you define "home" when your entire life is temporary? When you are constantly being uprooted, when your belongings are limited to a bag, and when uncertainty is your only certainty, what anchors you? Slowly, I began to see that for many people, home wasn't a physical place. It was a state of being, home was where they found themselves. That realization struck a chord deep within me. It wasn't just a theory. It became a guiding truth that I've lived through many times personally.

At Home in Transition became more than a design thesis. It became a human framework, one that supported people in vulnerable states of transit and helped them journey toward self-efficacy, and eventually, self-actualization. It was about recognizing the strength, talent, and potential in people even when they were at their most fragile. From there, we worked on pathways to empowerment: skill-building, entrepreneurship, and creating systems that transcended national borders.

The project culminated in my diploma, co-created with one of my best friends. But the real test came on the day of our defense. I remember being terrified. The project had such a deeply human core that I worried we hadn't delivered a "real" product. We hadn't developed an app. We hadn't built a sleek physical object. What we had created was a complex ecosystem of services, systems, and processes, tools designed not to impress, but to support real people on real journeys.

To our surprise, the room stood up and applauded.

It was in that moment I realized: we hadn't failed—we had, in fact, embodied the true power of human-centric design. We had built something that couldn't be boxed or coded but could be lived, felt, and evolved by the people it served.

Later, At Home in Transition would become my first EU-funded project and the foundation for the Euro-Nordic Funding Alliance, as mentioned previously, a network created to empower entrepreneurs with cross-border business development and financing.

This wasn't just a design project. It was a living example of how business and design can, and must, be built around people. Not personas. Not data points. But actual people, with talents and challenges, and the potential to thrive if only we design systems that truly see them.

I've always believed that great design begins with people. This philosophy was shaped early in my career, during projects where the stakes weren't just about delivering a product, they were about solving real problems for real people. One moment that stands out was during a systemic design workshop where we were mapping out a complex problem. We were deep into the process when a participant, a stakeholder who'd been quiet for most of the session, spoke up.

"This doesn't reflect what we experience day to day," they said, pointing to a part of the map. "It's missing how things actually work for us on the ground."

That comment changed everything. The insights we had painstakingly mapped out looked logical and thorough, but they weren't rooted in the lived realities of the people affected by the system. That moment drove home a critical lesson: without listening deeply to the people who interact with the systems, products, or services you're designing, even the most elegant solution will fall flat.

This chapter is about designing with empathy, prioritizing users and their needs at every stage. We'll explore how real-world applications of user-centered design have transformed startups and projects and how strategies like co-creation, feedback loops, and user research create meaningful, impactful solutions. Great design isn't about what we think works, it's about what truly works for the people we're designing for.

The Future of Business: Purpose as a System, Not a Slogan

We hear about "impact business" and "impact investment" so often that the words sometimes feel overused, almost emptied of meaning. But here's the truth: when you truly design for people and for the planet, not as an afterthought, not as a marketing slogan, but as the core of your process, business stops feeling like a tug-of-war between "doing good" and "doing well." It becomes a single, integrated system where profit and purpose fuel each other, and where success is measured not just by growth charts but by the change you create. A human-centric and environmental approach is not a moral accessory or a marketing tactic; it's a growth strategy, a risk strategy, and an innovation engine all at once.

Human-centric design starts with a humble question: what is it like to be them?

Not a persona in a PowerPoint deck, but an actual person living their actual life. That shift in perspective is what allowed GE Healthcare to transform pediatric MRI scans from a source of terror into an adventure.[40] The technology didn't change, the magnet was the same, but the experience was reimagined. Pirate ship decals, jungle cave sound effects, and playful nurse scripts turned a sterile procedure into a story children wanted to be part of. Sedation rates dropped, patient satisfaction soared, and hospital throughput improved. This is what happens when design is used not just to make something function, but to make it feel right.

The same was true for Bank of America's "Keep the Change" program.[41] Instead of telling people to become perfect savers, they designed a program that rounded up purchases and quietly tucked away the difference. It worked with human behavior rather than against it, which is why it scaled so quickly and became a signature product. Or consider M-Pesa in Kenya, which didn't set out to be a "fintech disruptor." It started with a basic human problem: people needed a safer way to move money where banks were scarce and cash was risky.[42] By using something everyone already had, a basic mobile phone, M-Pesa became not just a payment system but the foundation for a new kind of economy, connecting merchants, enabling remittances, and unlocking micro-loans.

Even in sectors as technical as healthcare delivery, human-centered design has been transformative. Mayo Clinic's SPARC innovation lab redesigned everything from waiting rooms to the language doctors used with patients.[43] They didn't just "add features"—they reimagined the entire journey, resulting in fewer dropped balls, clearer expectations, better patient outcomes, and more satisfied staff. When you design with empathy, you don't just improve experience—you improve operations.

The same principle applies to designing for the planet. True environmental design is not simply about swapping materials for greener ones; it's about rethinking the value chain so that the business gets stronger as waste goes down. Interface, the global carpet tile company, proved this with its "Mission Zero" initiative.[44] It redesigned everything, from materials to manufacturing, so that the company could eventually run on recycled and bio-based inputs. The outcome wasn't just lower carbon emissions; it became a competitive moat. As regulation tightened and customer expectations shifted, Interface was already ahead. Fairphone took a similar approach by building a modular smartphone designed for repairability and longevity. Their customers became advocates because they could replace a cracked screen or upgrade their battery instead of throwing away the entire device.

Too Good To Go turned food waste into a business model by connecting restaurants with surplus meals to customers through a simple app, profit came from preventing loss, not generating more consumption.[45] And d.light, along with M-KOPA, built a solar home system designed for pay-as-you-go micro-financing, aligning clean energy adoption with the cash flow realities of low-income households.[46]

Perhaps no brand has made the marriage of human and environmental design more visible than Patagonia. Their famous "Don't Buy This Jacket" campaign challenged customers to consume less, not more, and then backed that up with repair programs, durable materials, and an ownership structure that channels profits into climate initiatives.[47] Far from hurting sales, this honesty and alignment created one of the most loyal customer bases in the world. When you design for the planet, you're not just avoiding harm, you're creating resilience, reducing regulatory risk, and building a brand that customers and employees want to stand behind.

The most resilient companies now weave human and environmental value together from day one. Loop, a project by TerraCycle, reimagines consumer packaged goods by turning single-use packaging into a durable asset that can be returned, refilled, and reused.[48] Shoppers get a better experience, cities get cleaner waste streams, and brands get direct data on consumption patterns. Ecosia transforms a daily habit, web searching, into tree planting, funding reforestation through ad revenue. And at a city scale, Barcelona's "superblocks" redesigned streets not just to reduce car traffic but to create space for play, greenery, and social interaction. Air quality improved, local shops saw more foot traffic, and residents felt a renewed sense of community. Human benefit and planetary benefit reinforced each other.[49]

What ties all these examples together is a simple but powerful insight: businesses perform better when they are designed to fit the real world—its people, its ecosystems, and its limits. Human-centric and environmental design lower acquisition costs because customers love and recommend the product. They increase lifetime value because loyalty goes up. They derisk operations by reducing dependency on fragile supply chains and resource-intensive inputs. They prepare you for inevitable regulations and carbon pricing. And they turn your company into a magnet for top talent, because the best people want to work on something that matters.

If you want to practice this yourself, try an exercise: spend a day in your customer's life without selling or pitching anything, just watch. Notice the moments of friction, the tiny annoyances they've learned to tolerate. Fix one of those. Then take one of your top products and trace its materials all the way back to their source and forward to where they end up after use.

Circle one component you could substitute, eliminate, or loop back into a circular model this quarter. Imagine how your product could be repaired, refurbished, or reused instead of discarded. Test a take-back program for one product in one market. And don't just measure revenue, measure the impact you create for people and the planet, and let those metrics guide your design choices.

If you remember nothing else, remember this: human-centric and environmental design are not two separate projects. They are a single operating system for modern business. When you design this way, your product becomes something people love, your costs become smarter, your risks become smaller, and your brand becomes a story people are proud to share.

The future belongs to those who design for it, people, planet, and all. Every decision you make can be a vote for the world you want to see. So ask yourself: if your product disappeared tomorrow, would people fight to bring it back, and would the planet thank you for it?

Building with Empathy: How Design Prioritizes Users and Their Needs

Imagine being handed a tool you've never seen before and being expected to use it flawlessly. You fumble, try a few things, and eventually give up, muttering, "This wasn't made for me." That frustration, that feeling of being unseen or misunderstood, is exactly what empathetic design aims to eliminate.

Designing with empathy means understanding the world as your users experience it. It's about zooming in on their challenges, their habits, and even their small, everyday frustrations, and then designing solutions that seamlessly fit into their lives. At its heart, empathy in design is an act of respect, acknowledging that users are more than metrics; they're people with complex needs, behaviors, and emotions.

A New Way of Seeing

Empathy in design starts by reframing how you see your users. Instead of viewing them as end points in a process, you begin to see them as collaborators in creation. This perspective shift transforms the design process from one of assumptions to one of discovery.

I once worked on a project that aimed to streamline the onboarding process for new employees in a large organization. On paper, the system seemed efficient, step-by-step instructions, automated processes, and clear timelines.

But when we sat down with new hires and asked them to walk us through their experiences, the cracks became obvious. What was intuitive for the designers felt overwhelming and impersonal for the users. Their feedback wasn't about the technology; it was about the lack of human touch, something no amount of automation could replace. That experience taught me that empathy isn't about imagining what users might need; it's about listening until they tell you.

The Practices of Empathetic Design

Bringing empathy into the design process requires a set of intentional practices that go beyond surface-level user research. Here are some ways to make empathy a practical tool:

Be Present with Your Users

Empathy starts with being present. Spend time with your users in their environments, observing how they interact with the world. Watch how they work, ask them what frustrates them, and pay attention to the details they might not think to share.

Example: While designing an app for retail workers, shadowing employees on the shop floor revealed subtle pain points, like needing to switch screens constantly, that were never mentioned in feedback forms.

Ask Questions You Don't Think You Need to Ask

The best insights often come from questions that seem obvious. "Why do you do it this way?" or "What do you wish you could change?" are simple, open-ended questions that can uncover deep truths.

Realization: When interviewing users for a financial planning tool, we discovered that people weren't struggling with budgets, they were afraid of confronting their spending habits. That insight reshaped the entire design to focus on easing anxiety.

Humanize the Data

User research often gets distilled into statistics, charts, and personas. But behind every data point is a person with a story. Design teams that stay connected to those stories, whether through recorded interviews, user videos, or testimonials, design with more compassion and insight.

Empathy in Action: Real-World Transformations

Empathy isn't just a feel-good principle, it's a transformative tool. Some of the most successful startups and systems have empathy baked into their foundations.

The power of user-centered design lies in its ability to transform ideas into solutions that truly work for the people they're meant to serve. It's not a process confined to theory; it's a practice that has shaped some of the most impactful startups and projects. By focusing on users' needs, behaviors, and pain points, businesses can create products, systems, and services that go beyond functionality, they connect emotionally and solve real problems.

For example, when Nintendo set out to develop the Wii, they weren't just designing for hardcore gamers, they wanted to create something that could be enjoyed by everyone, from children to grandparents. This inclusive approach redefined what gaming could be.[50]

Challenges Identified:

Traditional gaming systems were intimidating to non-gamers due to complex controllers and mechanics.

The market was saturated with consoles targeting a narrow audience of experienced gamers.

Design Solutions:

Motion-Based Controls: The Wii's motion-sensitive controllers simplified gameplay, making it intuitive for players of all skill levels.

Inclusive Game Library: Nintendo designed games like Wii Sports that appealed to a wide audience, encouraging social play and physical activity.

User Testing: Extensive usability testing ensured that the controls were accessible to users of all ages and physical abilities.

Outcomes:

The Wii became one of the best-selling consoles of all time, with over 100 million units sold.

It expanded the gaming market, attracting millions of new players who had never engaged with video games before.

Another example is Ford Focus: Designing Vehicles for Accessibility. Ford's user-centered approach to redesigning the Focus included considering the needs of elderly drivers and those with physical limitations.[51] Their goal was to create a car that was not just functional but also accessible to a broader range of users.

Challenges Identified:

Traditional car designs often overlooked the needs of older drivers and those with mobility challenges.

Features like seat adjustments and control layouts were difficult for certain users to operate.

Design Solutions:

Empathy Tools: Engineers wore suits that simulated limited mobility to understand how users with physical constraints interacted with the vehicle.

Accessible Controls: The team redesigned seat adjustments, door handles, and dashboards to be more intuitive and ergonomic.

User Testing: Older drivers and people with disabilities were directly involved in the testing process.

Outcomes:

The redesign improved accessibility for all users, earning praise for its inclusivity.

Ford's innovative approach became a benchmark for user-centered design in the automotive industry.

These stories highlight the transformative power of user-centered design across diverse industries. By prioritizing the needs, behaviors, and emotions of their users, these companies were able to identify unique challenges and create solutions that not only met but exceeded expectations.

Whether it was simplifying complex gaming controllers, personalizing entertainment experiences, or redesigning vehicles for accessibility, the common thread in all these successes was empathy. User-centered design goes beyond solving problems, it redefines the relationship between people and the products or services they interact with, creating meaningful connections and lasting loyalty.

These examples serve as a reminder that when companies listen, observe, and innovate with their users in mind, they don't just grow, they transform industries and reshape experiences for millions worldwide.

The Ripple Effect of Empathy

Empathy doesn't just change what you design; it changes how you design. Teams that embrace empathetic practices collaborate better because they're focused on shared goals, helping people. Organizations that prioritize empathy build trust with their users, resulting in stronger relationships and greater loyalty. And designers who lead with empathy create solutions that don't just function but resonate.

When you design and build your business with empathy, you're not just solving problems, you're connecting with people in ways that matter. You're making them feel seen, heard, and valued. And in a world where people are often treated as statistics or data points, that connection is the most powerful design choice you can make.

In the world of innovation, assumptions are dangerous. They lead to products that no one uses, services that miss the mark, and businesses that fail to resonate with the people they're trying to reach. User research, feedback, and co-creation act as counterbalances to this tendency. They keep businesses honest, grounded, and aligned with the realities of their audiences.

Here's how to embed these practices into the heart of your business development process, step by step.

1. Begin with Context, Not Ideas

Every user exists within a context, a set of habits, preferences, and constraints that shape how they interact with your product or service. Before brainstorming solutions or sketching designs, immerse yourself in their world.

Practical Approach:

Spend time in the environments where your users live or work. Observe how they interact with similar products or services.

Ask specific, situational questions: "How do you currently solve this problem?" or "What do you do when this happens?"

Side Tip #1: Contextual research often reveals latent needs, problems users might not articulate but that still affect them deeply.

2. Treat Feedback as a Starting Line, Not a Finish Line

Feedback is most valuable when it sparks exploration. Too often, businesses treat feedback as binary approval or rejection. Instead, use it to uncover deeper insights.

Practical Approach:

When users say, "This doesn't work for me," follow up with, "Can you tell me why?"

Analyze patterns across feedback. A single comment might seem minor, but repeated observations can point to systemic issues.

Side Tip #2: Create a "Why Five Times" feedback loop. For every piece of feedback, ask "why" up to five times to drill down to the root cause.

3. Prototype for Discovery, Not Perfection

Your first prototype is a question, not an answer. The goal isn't to prove you're right but to discover what works and what doesn't.

Practical Approach:

Start small. A sketch, a clickable wireframe, or a quick role-play exercise can reveal critical insights without heavy investment.

Test in diverse scenarios. If your product works in a crowded café, a quiet office, and on a bumpy bus ride, it's ready for the real world.

Side Tip #3: Test with extreme users, people whose needs deviate significantly from the norm. Designing for extremes often creates solutions that work better for everyone.

4. Make Co-Creation a Mindset, Not a Meeting

Co-creation isn't just a workshop activity; it's a way of thinking about design. When you treat users as partners, you unlock perspectives you'd never reach alone.

Practical Approach:

Involve users at every stage, from ideation to testing. Let them brainstorm with you, critique your prototypes, and suggest alternatives.

Use collaborative tools like Miro or MURAL to create virtual spaces where users can contribute ideas.

Side Tip #4: Rotate your user panel to avoid over-relying on the same perspectives. Fresh voices keep insights diverse and relevant.

5. Use Metrics to Validate, Not Dictate

Metrics are powerful, but they're not infallible. Use them to inform decisions, but don't let them override user insights or intuition.

Practical Approach:

Pair qualitative and quantitative data. For instance, track how users engage with a feature (quantitative) and ask them why they use it that way (qualitative).

Look for leading indicators of success, like user retention or repeat usage, rather than lagging metrics like revenue.

Side Tip #5: Avoid "vanity metrics" that look good on paper but don't reflect real user value. Focus on actionable insights.

6. Build Feedback Channels Into Your Product

Don't wait for users to tell you what they think, invite their input directly through your product or service.

Practical Approach:

Add simple feedback mechanisms like "Was this helpful?" buttons, comment fields, or satisfaction sliders.

Use periodic pop-ups or emails to request input without being intrusive.

Side Tip #6: Close the loop by showing users how their feedback influenced your decisions. It builds trust and encourages more engagement.

Design is at its most powerful when it becomes an act of listening. These exercises aren't just tasks, they're doorways into the lives of your users, offering you a chance to understand their joys, frustrations, and unmet needs. Imagine stepping into their shoes, walking through their daily routines, and realizing that the solutions you create could ease their burdens or spark a smile.

This isn't about checking off a to-do list. It's about curiosity. It's about letting go of your assumptions and being surprised by what you find. When you approach design with empathy and humility, you don't just create products, you create experiences that matter. So, step forward, lean in, and let your users show you what's possible.

Exercise: User-Centric Entrepreneurs

These thoughtful exercises are designed to immerse you in the principles of empathy, user-centered design, and co-creation. Each one encourages deep reflection and meaningful application without overwhelming your time.

1. The Invisible Struggles Challenge

Spend 30 minutes observing someone interacting with a product or service similar to yours. Focus on their body language, subtle frustrations, and unspoken actions.

- Write down three observations where they seemed to struggle or improvise.
- Reflect on how your product or service could address these hidden pain points.

Purpose: To uncover challenges that users often don't verbalize but deeply affect their experience.

2. Create a User's Emotional Map

Pick a specific interaction that your users have with your product or service.

- Map their emotions at each stage (e.g., confusion, relief, frustration, delight).
- Highlight one negative emotion and brainstorm a way to transform it into a positive one.

Purpose: To focus on the emotional impact of your design and refine it for a better user experience.

3. Co-Design in 15 Minutes

Invite one user to a quick co-creation session.

- Present a challenge or feature you're working on.
- Brainstorm solutions together, letting the user sketch, critique, or refine ideas with you.

Purpose: To foster collaboration and uncover ideas you might not have considered alone.

Final Challenge

Take an existing feature or service from your business and redesign it using these three steps:

- Observe users interacting with it.
- Incorporate their feedback into one meaningful change.
- Test the updated version and note the impact.

Goal: To apply user-centered design principles to a tangible part of your business and reflect on how it improves the experience for your users.

Design is at its most powerful when it becomes an act of listening. The exercises above aren't just tasks, they're doorways into the lives of your users, offering you a chance to understand their joys, frustrations, and unmet needs. Imagine stepping into their shoes, walking through their daily routines, and realizing that the solutions you create could ease their burdens or spark a smile.

This isn't about checking off a to-do list. It's about curiosity. It's about letting go of your assumptions and being surprised by what you find. When you approach design with empathy and humility, you don't just create products, you create experiences that matter. So, step forward, lean in, and let your users show you what's possible.

Chapter 10:
Bias, Barriers, and Bridges

Well, I can't write a book about business and not talk about this!

Speaking of culture and adaptation, being a woman in business, especially in the context of migration, is a masterclass in resilience and dealing with complexity. It's not just about navigating new markets or learning new languages; it's about constantly renegotiating who you are allowed to be.

Each culture, each country, each boardroom has its own unspoken rules for how women should show up, lead, and speak. And as a female founder, I have had to learn how to read those rules, break them when necessary, and design new ones where none existed.

Contrary to the image often painted of Iranian women as powerless, I grew up surrounded by women who were anything but. I was surrounded by women who built businesses out of their living rooms, led NGOs in remote villages, and ran schools that educated children others had forgotten. I saw women take the driver's seat—literally—forming Iran's first female racing and motocross teams. They strapped on helmets, revved their engines, and tore through the dirt, rewriting what society said was "acceptable." These women didn't just break barriers—they turned those barriers into fuel, reshaping the rules entirely. My mother was one of them.

A social entrepreneur with unshakable resolve, she built youth libraries that became sanctuaries for kids after school and ran financial independence programs for women in rural areas. I watched her navigate societal scrutiny with quiet strength, balancing cultural expectations while empowering women to dismantle those very constraints.

That's what Iran gave me: strength forged in fire. When systems try to box women in, we learn how to push, bend, and innovate.

So when I moved to Norway, I thought I was stepping into freedom—and in many ways, I was. I could speak openly, choose what to wear, live independently. But freedom there came with its own set of barriers.

The oppression wasn't loud or obvious. It was quiet, polite, and bureaucratic. For me as an immigrant founder, every form, every process felt like a test. Did I know the unspoken rules? Could I decode the language? Did I fit the mold of the "right" kind of founder?

This was systemic oppression of a different kind, not driven by ideology, but by the weight of structure. And yet, just as in Iran, I found a way through. I leaned on design as my superpower. I stopped resisting the system and started mapping it, identifying leverage points, nudging it where it could bend. I learned who to talk to, how to align my ventures with existing structures, and how to build allies who opened doors instead of closing them.

But through all of this, one of the deepest challenges I've seen, both in myself and in other women founders, is the temptation to erase parts of ourselves just to be taken seriously. I've met countless brilliant women who downplayed their femininity, muted their voices, or even rejected their womanhood to "fit in."

And I understand why, society often rewards us when we stop taking up space as women and start blending into the existing mold.

But I've learned that this comes at a cost. Running away from who we are is not empowerment, it's self-erasure. It's another kind of cage.

For years, I lived with labels: "immigrant," "female founder," "Iranian entrepreneur." For a long time, the anger those labels sparked was fuel, it pushed me to work harder, to prove I belonged. But anger can only carry you so far. Today, my drive comes from something deeper: purpose, faith, and a commitment to create systems that outlast me.

That's why I want to be known simply as an entrepreneur. Not a "female entrepreneur." Not an "immigrant founder." Just an entrepreneur, whose work speaks louder than her labels. This doesn't mean that networks and initiatives championing women aren't important, on the contrary, they are essential stepping stones. But their purpose shouldn't end at creating a comfortable space to sympathize over shared struggles.

The real goal is to equip women to actively practice the world they want to belong to, one where leadership is inclusive by default, and the label "female founder" becomes unnecessary because women in leadership are no longer the exception but simply the norm.

Women under oppression don't just break, they adapt, evolve, and grow stronger. And when we bring that strength into entrepreneurship, it becomes a superpower.

Design-driven entrepreneurship, in particular, gives us the tools to see the systems clearly, to map the barriers, and to redesign the paths forward—not just for ourselves, but for the women who come after us.

That's what this journey has taught me: leadership isn't about becoming someone else to be accepted.

It's about bringing your whole self to the table, your culture, your femininity, your resilience, and building ventures that reflect all of it. Because when we lead from that place of authenticity, we stop just surviving in the system—we start reshaping it.

Addressing Gender Biases and Stereotypes in the Entrepreneurial Ecosystem

Let's be honest, when people hear "entrepreneur," many still imagine a tech-savvy guy in a hoodie, pitching his startup while sipping cold brew in a minimalist co-working space. But what happens when the entrepreneur doesn't fit this narrow mold? What if she's a woman?

Suddenly, the stereotypes come rushing in, sometimes subtle, sometimes loud, but always present.

Here are a few of my "favorites" (read: least favorite) gender biases women entrepreneurs encounter, and how we can flip the script.

Bias #1: "Women aren't risk-takers."

Ah yes, the old "men take the risks, women play it safe" trope. The irony here is that entrepreneurship is practically a synonym for risk, and women have been doing it for centuries, whether it's launching businesses, managing families, or fighting for equal rights.

The Flip:

Research shows that women often take calculated risks, balancing bold decisions with careful planning. This isn't about avoiding risk, it's about ensuring risks are strategic and sustainable.

Example: Sara Blakely, the founder of Spanx, started her billion-dollar company by risking her savings to patent and prototype her product. [52]

Calculated? Yes.

Safe? Definitely not.

Bias #2: "Women are too emotional to lead."

This one is a classic. The idea that showing emotion undermines leadership is as outdated as dial-up internet. Women are often perceived as "too emotional," while men with the same level of passion are called "charismatic" or "visionary."

The Flip:

Emotional intelligence (EQ) is one of the most sought-after leadership qualities today, and women tend to score higher on EQ metrics. Empathy, adaptability, and relationship-building are essential for leading teams and businesses.

Example: Oprah Winfrey's empathetic leadership style didn't just build her media empire, it made her one of the most trusted figures in the world.

Bias #3: "Women don't understand the numbers."

The assumption here is that women lack the analytical skills to handle complex finances or scale a business. Spoiler alert: women not only understand the numbers, they often outperform their male counterparts.

The Flip:

Numerous studies have shown that companies with women in leadership positions often achieve higher profitability and return on investment. Women-led ventures are more likely to prioritize long-term sustainability over short-term gains.

Example: Indra Nooyi, former CEO of PepsiCo, led the company through a period of record-breaking growth by combining sharp financial strategies with sustainable initiatives.[53]

Bias #4: "Women's businesses are 'lifestyle' businesses."

This one suggests that women are more likely to start businesses as a hobby or side hustle rather than serious ventures. It overlooks the countless women who have built transformative companies while balancing a million other roles.

The Flip:

Women are founders of some of the fastest-growing startups globally, and their businesses span every industry, from technology to healthcare.

Example: Whitney Wolfe Herd founded Bumble, a dating app that went public with a valuation of $13 billion, definitely not your average "lifestyle" business.[54]

Bias #5: "Investors are just more comfortable with male founders."

This is one of the most damaging biases. Studies show that female entrepreneurs receive less than 3% of venture capital funding globally.[55] Investors are often unconsciously influenced by stereotypes, asking women founders questions about risk mitigation while asking men about growth potential.

The Flip:

Change is happening, albeit slowly. Female-focused VC funds, like Female Founders Fund and Backstage Capital, are rewriting the narrative by prioritizing investments in women-led startups. These ventures aren't just succeeding, they're thriving.

Example: Stitch Fix, founded by Katrina Lake, became a publicly traded company and demonstrated the massive potential of women-led innovation.

How to Bust These Biases

If you're an entrepreneur facing these stereotypes, remember: the best way to challenge a bias is to succeed in spite of it, and to build systems that support others to do the same. Here's how we can all help:

1. Call Out the Bias:
Whether you're in a meeting or at a pitch event, don't let stereotypes slide. Gently but firmly address biased comments, pointing out data or examples that challenge them.

2. Redefine Success Stories:
Celebrate the stories of women who've smashed stereotypes and succeeded on their own terms. These narratives are powerful tools for changing perceptions.

3. Design Inclusive Systems:
Investors, accelerators, and mentors can create spaces that actively encourage diversity, by questioning their own assumptions, funding women-led ventures, and fostering inclusive networks.

Gender biases don't define us, but how we respond to them does. Women in entrepreneurship are already rewriting the script, proving that the only thing more outdated than these stereotypes is the belief that they'll hold us back. Let's leave the biases in the dust and keep building a future where success isn't about fitting a mold, it's about breaking it.

The Role of Design in Navigating Cultural Complexities and Empowering Diverse Founders

Imagine you're building a bridge, but the two sides you're trying to connect speak completely different languages. One side prefers efficiency and directness; the other values relationships and context. Without understanding both, your bridge might look great but fail to hold any weight.

This is what cultural complexity often feels like in entrepreneurship—an intricate web of unspoken rules, assumptions, and expectations. But here's the good news: design isn't just about products or services; it's a superpower for solving these challenges. When done right, design doesn't just navigate cultural complexities—it thrives on them, turning differences into strengths and empowering founders to lead with confidence and authenticity.

1. Start with Cultural Empathy

The first step in design is to listen. Not to reply, not to fix, but to understand. Diverse founders often operate in systems that weren't built for them, and their insights into cultural dynamics are invaluable.

Practical Tip: Conduct cultural audits when designing systems or products. Ask questions like:

- How do people communicate in this context?
- What values are prioritized (e.g., hierarchy, community, or individualism)?
- Are there cultural taboos or sensitivities to consider?

Example:

In one project for a global workforce platform, user testing revealed that what felt like "straightforward communication" to users in one region came across as abrupt or even rude in another. By redesigning workflows to incorporate cultural nuance, the platform improved adoption rates across multiple markets.

2. Use Design to Create Inclusive Spaces

Whether it's a physical workspace or a virtual platform, the environments we design should make everyone feel like they belong. Diverse founders often find themselves excluded from traditional networks, but design can level the playing field.

Practical Tip:

- In Physical Spaces: Use universal design principles to make environments welcoming. Consider accessibility, lighting, layout, and cultural symbols that reflect inclusivity.
- In Digital Platforms: Allow users to customize their experience, language options, cultural themes, and flexible workflows can make platforms feel more personal.

Example:

Co-working spaces like The Wing (before its rebranding) succeeded in creating environments tailored to women founders by incorporating thoughtful design elements such as private nursing rooms, diverse artwork, and inclusive programming.

3. Turn Cultural Complexity into a Design Asset

Every culture brings unique problem-solving approaches, perspectives, and values. Instead of viewing these differences as barriers, design systems that harness them.

Practical Tip:

- Facilitate cross-cultural workshops where teams share how they approach challenges. Use these insights to design systems that incorporate multiple perspectives.
- Apply modular design principles: create flexible frameworks that can adapt to cultural nuances rather than imposing one-size-fits-all solutions.

Example:

Lego embraced cultural complexity by involving children and parents from various regions in the design of its toys.[56] This led to product lines that respected diverse play styles and preferences, making Lego a global brand with universal appeal.

4. Empower Founders to Design Authentically

For diverse founders, the pressure to conform to dominant cultural norms can be exhausting. Design systems and narratives that celebrate authenticity rather than forcing founders to fit a mold.

Practical Tip:

- Design pitch decks, workshops, or accelerator programs that prioritize storytelling over buzzwords. Let founders lead with their unique perspectives and experiences.
- Provide tools for self-expression, like branding guides or templates, that help founders articulate their vision in a way that feels authentic to them.

Example:

Bumble's founder, Whitney Wolfe Herd, leaned into her personal values to design a dating app that prioritized women's agency and safety. By embedding those principles into every aspect of the platform, she created a business that felt both authentic and revolutionary.

5. Build Systems for Cultural Awareness

Cultural blind spots often emerge in systems that weren't designed with diversity in mind. By embedding cultural awareness into your design processes, you can create systems that anticipate and navigate complexity.

Practical Tip:

- Incorporate cultural training into team onboarding, helping everyone understand the dynamics of the markets or communities you serve.
- Use design tools like GIGA-mapping to visualize cultural touchpoints and identify areas where misunderstandings might arise.

Example:

Airbnb's global success relied heavily on understanding cultural differences. For instance, in Japan, they redesigned their approach to highlight host etiquette and cleanliness, addressing cultural priorities and building trust in the market.

6. Celebrate the Strength of Diverse Teams

Diverse teams don't just navigate cultural complexities, they create better solutions. When founders and teams bring different cultural perspectives to the table, the result is often more innovative, inclusive, and impactful.

Practical Tip:

- Use design thinking exercises to encourage collaboration, ensuring every voice is heard.
- Celebrate milestones that reflect cultural values, whether it's launching a product or simply recognizing holidays and traditions within the team.

Example:

When Slack built its emoji library, they included culturally diverse icons and symbols, ensuring that the platform resonated with its global user base. This small but significant design choice strengthened its appeal across cultures.[57]

When we design with cultural nuance and inclusivity, we don't just solve problems—we create opportunities, spark innovation, and build a world where everyone has a seat at the table. And who doesn't want to be part of that kind of world?

Personal Experiences and Insights into Creating Inclusive Systems and Narratives

I was once at a roundtable discussion where everyone introduced themselves with their titles. The room felt heavy with formality, CEOs, VCs, Directors. When it was my turn, I decided to break the mold. "I'm Nilu," I said, "a designer who's obsessed with fixing systems that don't work for everyone." A few people smiled, others looked slightly confused, and one person leaned forward and said, *"What does that mean?"*

That question became the spark for a conversation that turned into a lesson. As I explained my approach, blending design, entrepreneurship, and empathy to create systems where everyone feels like they belong, I saw people start to connect, not just with the idea but with each other. The rigid atmosphere softened. Titles faded into the background, and stories emerged.

One founder talked about the isolation they felt as the only woman in a male-dominated industry. Another shared the challenges of pitching their idea in a market that didn't value their cultural perspective. By the end of the session, it was clear: creating inclusive systems isn't just about policies or platforms, it's about changing the stories we tell and the spaces we create.

For me, designing inclusive systems starts with listening. Not just to what people say but to what they leave unsaid, the silences that often speak louder than words. It's about asking the hard questions: Who isn't in the room? Whose voice isn't being heard? What assumptions are we making without realizing it?

In one project, I worked with a diverse team of entrepreneurs to design a program for first-time founders. We didn't just build a curriculum; we built trust. We created spaces where people felt safe to share their vulnerabilities, their ideas, and their fears. We rewrote the narrative from "you're here to compete" to "you're here to collaborate."

That experience taught me that inclusion isn't a checkbox; it's a culture. It's in the stories we tell about success, the way we structure conversations, and the systems we design to ensure that everyone has a chance to thrive. It's not about erasing differences but celebrating them, recognizing that diversity isn't just a challenge to overcome, it's the wellspring of innovation.

When we design inclusively, we don't just make systems better. We make people feel seen, valued, and empowered. And in the end, isn't that what entrepreneurship is all about?

Bonus Exercise: Leadership for Female Founders

Being a female founder isn't about proving you can do it "just like the men." It's about defining leadership on your own terms, leading with authenticity, not apology.

Step 1 – Your Leadership Words:
Choose three words that describe the leader you aspire to be. Write them somewhere you can see every day.

Step 2 – Your Story of Strength:
Reflect on a moment where you broke through a cultural or professional barrier. What inner strength got you through? Write a one-paragraph story about it— it's part of your founder DNA.

Step 3 – Create Your Circle:
List three women you admire (alive or dead, local or global). What do they have in common? What lessons from their journeys can you weave into your own?

Step 4 – Pass It On:
Leadership grows through connection. Identify one woman in your network you could support, through mentorship, collaboration, or simply encouragement. Take one concrete step this month.

Step 5 – Visualize Your Future Team:
Sketch or describe the culture you want to create. How do you want your team to feel on Monday mornings? How will your values show up in the way decisions are made?

Chapter 11:
Designing Teams that Innovate

I remember standing in the pit before one of my races, watching the team around me move like an orchestra. The engineers were tweaking the engine map, the mechanics were making micro-adjustments to tire pressure, the strategist was recalculating fuel loads based on weather forecasts, and the physiotherapist reminded me to hydrate and stay calm.

It struck me then: racing isn't just about speed, it's about systems. Every detail, every discipline matters, and when they align, magic happens.

In one race, for instance, the weather turned halfway through, sudden rain on an otherwise dry track. My instinct as a driver told me to push, but the strategist's call came through the radio: pit now. In the few seconds it took to swap tires, the mechanics executed flawlessly, and the engineers recalibrated on the fly. I went back out and gained positions not because I was the fastest on the track, but because the team had designed the right system around me. Strategy, physics, mechanics, human intuition, they all came together in that moment.

That experience has stayed with me far beyond the track. It showed me that creativity and performance aren't about waiting for the perfect idea or moment, they're about building environments where disciplines collide, where every perspective counts, and where the system itself becomes the driver of innovation.

Techniques for Nurturing Creativity in Interdisciplinary Teams

When you gather a group of people from different disciplines, you're essentially inviting a symphony of perspectives to solve problems in ways no single expertise could achieve alone.

But blending those perspectives into creative harmony isn't automatic, it requires intention, structure, and a little bit of magic. Here are practical techniques for fostering creativity in interdisciplinary teams.

1. Create a Shared Language

Interdisciplinary teams often struggle with jargon. What's clear to an architect might sound like gibberish to a software engineer. Creating a shared language ensures everyone can communicate effectively, leveling the playing field and sparking richer collaboration.

How to Do It:

Glossaries: Develop a shared glossary of key terms at the beginning of a project.

Metaphors: Use metaphors and visual storytelling to explain complex ideas. For instance, a data scientist might explain an algorithm using the metaphor of a recipe.

Mapping Tools: Use visual tools like mind maps or flowcharts to represent ideas without relying on text-heavy explanations.

2. Build Psychological Safety

If people don't feel safe sharing their ideas, creativity will wither. In interdisciplinary teams, this fear can be amplified because of perceived hierarchies or lack of familiarity with other fields.

How to Do It:

Normalize "Bad" Ideas: Begin brainstorming sessions by encouraging wild, impractical ideas to set a playful tone.

No Interruption Rule: Ensure every person's contribution is heard without interruption.

Leader Vulnerability: If you're leading the team, admit what you don't know. This openness sets the tone for others to do the same.

3. Design for Structured Chaos

Creativity thrives in a space where structure and freedom coexist. Too much structure stifles innovation, while too much freedom leads to chaos. Strike a balance by setting boundaries that encourage exploration without overwhelming the team.

How to Do It:

Time-Boxed Brainstorms: Give the team 20 minutes to come up with as many ideas as possible, followed by a focused discussion to evaluate them.

Challenge Cards: Use prompts to inspire thinking in new directions. For example, "How would you solve this problem with no budget?" or "What if you could only use recycled materials?"

Rotating Roles: Rotate leadership roles during sessions, allowing different perspectives to guide the process.

4. Encourage Cross-Pollination of Ideas

Interdisciplinary teams are goldmines for creativity because they bring diverse expertise to the table. But those ideas only spark when people truly engage with perspectives outside their own.

How to Do It:

Reverse Mentorship: Pair team members from vastly different disciplines and have them explain their work to each other.

Field Trips: Organize team outings to places that inspire new thinking, a museum, a startup incubator, or even a factory floor.

Mix It Up: Change seating arrangements regularly to encourage conversations between disciplines that wouldn't normally interact.

5. Use Prototypes as Conversation Starters

Sometimes, words fall short in interdisciplinary teams. Prototypes, no matter how rough—act as tangible tools for discussion, helping teams align their ideas and refine their vision.

How to Do It:

Low-Fidelity Models: Use sketches, mockups, or even Lego to build quick representations of ideas.

Iterative Prototypes: Create prototypes in stages, allowing the team to see progress and suggest changes along the way.

User Involvement: Test prototypes with end-users and bring their feedback into the team's discussions.

6. Celebrate Diverse Thinking

Creativity flourishes when team members feel valued for their unique perspectives. Actively celebrating differences creates an atmosphere where people are motivated to contribute their best ideas.

How to Do It:

Highlight Unique Contributions: Acknowledge and thank team members for bringing insights from their field.

Diverse Inspiration Boards: Create shared inspiration boards where team members can pin ideas, images, or concepts from their discipline that relate to the project.

Cultural Inclusion: Incorporate cultural traditions or practices into team rituals, such as sharing stories or celebrating milestones.

Interdisciplinary teams are messy, unpredictable, and often challenging to manage, but they're also where the most extraordinary ideas are born. By intentionally nurturing creativity through shared language, psychological safety, structured chaos, and other strategies, you create a space where ideas flourish and innovation thrives.

When you build a team that not only tolerates but celebrates differences, you're not just solving problems, you're designing solutions that are richer, bolder, and more impactful than you ever thought possible.

Encouraging Experimentation and Risk-Taking

Experimentation and risk-taking are the lifeblood of creativity and innovation. They are about creating a space where failure isn't just tolerated but actively embraced as a critical part of growth and discovery. This isn't just a nice-to-have; it's essential for any team or organization that wants to thrive in a rapidly changing world.

Why Experimentation Matters

In a world where the only constant is change, sticking to tried-and-true methods isn't enough. Experimentation allows teams to venture beyond the obvious, test new ideas, and uncover unexpected solutions. Think of it as planting seeds: not every seed will grow, but some will sprout into something remarkable.

As a design-driven entrepreneur, I've seen how fostering a culture of experimentation can transform teams. When employees are encouraged to test their ideas, no matter how unconventional, they feel empowered and invested in the outcomes. This leads to breakthroughs that might never have been discovered in a rigid, risk-averse environment.

The Role of Risk-Taking

Risk-taking goes hand-in-hand with experimentation. To innovate, teams must be willing to step into the unknown, challenge the status quo, and make bold decisions. This doesn't mean taking reckless risks but calculated ones, grounded in research, empathy, and an openness to learn from failure.

Creating a Safe Space for Failure

One of the greatest barriers to experimentation and risk-taking is the fear of failure. As leaders and innovators, it's our job to reframe failure not as the opposite of success, but as a stepping stone to it. This involves:

Leading by Example: Share your own failures and the lessons learned from them.

Rewarding Boldness: Celebrate attempts and risks, even if they don't pan out.

Encouraging Reflection: After every experiment, analyze what worked, what didn't, and why.

From Theory to Practice

In my ventures, I've implemented a few strategies to embed experimentation and risk-taking into team culture:

1. Design Sprints: Rapid, time-bound challenges where teams test ideas with low-cost prototypes.

2. Fail-Forward Fridays: A space to share lessons from failures, turning them into teachable moments.

3. Creative Constraints: Set challenges with specific limitations to spark unconventional thinking.

These practices create an environment where creativity thrives and innovation becomes second nature.

The Payoff

Encouraging experimentation and risk-taking doesn't just lead to better ideas; it fosters resilience, adaptability, and a deeper sense of collaboration. Teams that feel safe to explore and take risks are not only more innovative but also more united and engaged in their work. In the end, embracing experimentation and risk-taking is about creating a culture where curiosity drives action, and every failure brings a step closer to success.

Building a Culture of Collaboration and Adaptability

Building a culture of collaboration and adaptability is like constructing a suspension bridge, each component has a role, each tension holds balance, and together they span uncharted waters. Collaboration is the sturdy cables, pulling ideas and efforts together, while adaptability forms the flexible deck that bends and adjusts to the shifting load of challenges and change. Together, they create a pathway where progress meets resilience.

Collaboration: The Strength in Unity

Collaboration is the process of weaving different materials into something stronger. When every individual brings their unique perspective, skill, and creativity to the table, the collective becomes capable of what no single person could achieve alone. This is not about agreeing on everything, it's about building bridges between ideas, finding common ground, and learning from the differences.

Adaptability: The Resilient Framework

Adaptability ensures the bridge doesn't break under pressure. It's the willingness to pivot, to reimagine the structure when storms come, or to reroute when the original path no longer serves. Adaptability allows teams to thrive in uncertainty, evolving with the demands of the moment while staying anchored to their purpose.

A Bridge Built to Last

When collaboration and adaptability converge, they create a team culture that doesn't just survive challenges, it grows stronger because of them. It's the kind of culture where people are not afraid to take risks, where ideas are tested without fear of failure, and where the focus remains on moving forward, no matter how turbulent the waters below.

A culture of collaboration and adaptability is not built overnight, but it's worth every effort. It's about constructing something enduring, something that enables people to traverse obstacles together, steady and flexible, with a shared vision of the other side. Build this, and your team won't just cross bridges, they'll create them.

You'll Only Be a Good Team Member If You Stay True to Yourself

One of the most transformative things I learned while working at DNB—yes, the same DNB we referred to earlier in the book—was that self-awareness isn't just personal growth, it's a professional asset.

After working with multiple teams and on countless cross-disciplinary projects, I began to notice patterns. Not just in the way others worked, but in the way I worked. I realized I had habits, tendencies, and quirks that either fueled or frustrated collaboration, depending on how well they were understood by those around me. So I started creating something like a guide called "How to Work with Nilu"—a short, five-page PowerPoint that I shared with every new person I worked with. And honestly, it changed everything.

This little guide became like a personal operations manual. It helped cut through so much unnecessary friction. Instead of spending weeks figuring out each other's styles, the people I worked with got a head start. They knew upfront what helped me thrive—and what might trip us up if we didn't talk about it. It was in fact a perfect ice-breaker with my new colleagues too.

One of the slides said something like, "If we're rehearsing a presentation and I completely mess it up, don't panic." I explained that I have ADHD, and that rehearsals without real audience energy throw me off balance. I often need the pressure of the moment to perform at my best. I draw energy from people, from the room, from improvisation. So if it looks like it's falling apart in rehearsal, it probably isn't. Trust me to land it.

Another point explained my fidgeting during meetings. I wrote that if I'm drawing in a notebook, fiddling with something, or glancing at my phone, it's not because I'm distracted or disrespectful. It's because I am paying attention, and that movement helps me listen better. Keeping my hands busy helps quiet the rest of the noise in my brain so I can focus.

These might sound like small things, but in a fast-paced work environment, they make a huge difference. By being open about how my mind works, I wasn't just asking for understanding, I was offering others a shortcut to collaborate better with me. And it created a space where others could be open too.

So I genuinely recommend this to everyone, especially in teams, small or big. Reflect on what you've learned about yourself by working with others. Capture it. It doesn't have to be formal or perfect. Just think of it as a guide you wish people had the first time they worked with you. What helps you focus? What frustrates you? How do you process feedback? What makes you feel heard? What throws you off course?

We often expect teamwork to just work, as if good intentions alone are enough. But working together is a design process too. It takes thought, iteration, and a lot of self-awareness. The best teams I've ever been part of weren't the ones with the flashiest titles or the most experience. They were the ones where people showed up as themselves, and were allowed to.

And that starts by knowing yourself well enough to share your blueprint with others.

1. The Shared Map

Create a shared map of your team's goals, contributions, and challenges. Each member adds their perspective on how they can contribute and adapt to shifting priorities. Use it to identify overlaps and opportunities for collaboration.

2. Scenario Shift

Pose a "what-if" scenario: "What if the deadline moved up by a month?" or "What if we had to deliver this project in half the budget?" Work together to brainstorm solutions. This strengthens adaptability and highlights each member's problem-solving approach.

3. Build the Bridge

Assign a team project where the goal is to create a solution with significant input from every member. Set a constraint that forces adaptation, such as using limited resources or adhering to a new framework.

4. Reflection Rounds

At the end of a project, hold a reflection session. Discuss: What collaboration methods worked best? Where did we adapt well, and where did we struggle? Use this to refine team practices.

5. Rotating Perspectives

For one task, have team members temporarily switch roles. This exercise fosters empathy, reveals interdependencies, and encourages collaborative problem-solving from new angles.

By practicing these strategies, you'll not only build bridges over today's challenges but also prepare your team to span tomorrow's uncertainties with strength and agility.

Side note: Now, I'm not only giving you exercises, but I'm involving your whole team! It's fun!

Practical Tools and Frameworks for Fostering Creativity in Teams

Creativity doesn't happen by accident, it happens by design.

In organizations that consistently innovate, creative output isn't the result of a few brilliant individuals; it's the product of intentionally crafted environments, rituals, and frameworks that invite curiosity, psychological safety, and experimentation.

Below are practical tools and frameworks that leaders and teams can use to unlock collective creativity and turn ideas into action.

1. The Creative Climate Canvas

Before generating ideas, teams need the right conditions to do so.

The Creative Climate Canvas helps you assess the current environment and identify what's enabling or limiting creative flow.

How to use it:

- On a large board (physical or digital), create five sections:
- Purpose – Do we share a clear "why" behind our work?
- Psychological Safety – Can people speak openly, take risks, and admit uncertainty?
- Diversity of Thought – Are we hearing multiple perspectives and disciplines?
- Resources – Do we have the time, tools, and data to explore?
- Rituals – What regular practices support creativity (or unintentionally block it)?

Reflection:

Invite the team to rate each area on a scale from 1–5. Discuss what's missing. The goal isn't blame, it's awareness. A creative culture begins when people see the system they're part of.

2. The "Problem Reframe" Framework

Innovation rarely starts with answers—it starts with better questions.

This framework helps teams pause before solution-mode and reexamine their challenge through different lenses.

Steps:

• State the problem plainly.

 Example: "Our onboarding process is too slow."

• Ask reframing questions:

What if the problem is actually the symptom of something deeper?

Who defines "slow," and why does it matter?

How would this problem look if we viewed it from the customer's or competitor's perspective?

• Rephrase the challenge as a "How Might We" question:

"How might we design an onboarding experience that feels effortless and empowering for new users?"

Why it works:

Reframing expands the field of possibility and helps teams uncover insights hiding beneath surface-level frustrations.

3. Diverge–Converge Cycles

A core principle of design thinking, diverge–converge cycles structure the creative process so teams can explore widely and then focus effectively.

How it works:

• Diverge: Generate as many ideas as possible, quantity over quality. No filtering.

• Cluster: Group similar ideas into themes or directions.

• Converge: Narrow to a few that align with purpose, feasibility, and impact.

Tip:

Run these cycles in short bursts. A well-facilitated 45-minute session can yield more insight than a week of unstructured brainstorming.

Tool pairing:

Use digital whiteboards like Miro, FigJam, or Notion to make thinking visible and inclusive, especially in hybrid or remote teams.

4. The Rapid Experiment Loop

The best teams don't just think creatively, they learn creatively.

The Rapid Experiment Loop is a lightweight approach to turning ideas into testable prototypes quickly.

Cycle:

- Hypothesize: "If we do X, users will respond by Y."
- Prototype: Build a simple version—paper, slide deck, or demo.
- Test: Share it with real users or peers.
- Learn: What worked? What surprised you?
- Adapt: Refine the idea or pivot completely.

Each loop should take no more than one week. Creativity grows stronger when it's exercised frequently, not saved for big moments.

5. The Creative Roles Model

Teams thrive when creativity is distributed, not concentrated.

This model helps members recognize the different roles that fuel creative progress.

Common creative roles include:

- The Explorer: Brings in new insights, trends, and analogies.
- The Synthesizer: Connects dots between disparate ideas.
- The Challenger: Questions assumptions and provokes new thinking.
- The Maker: Turns concepts into tangible prototypes.
- The Integrator: Aligns creative ideas with business and user goals.

In your next project, have each team member self-identify their primary and secondary roles.

Encourage rotation, today's "Explorer" might be tomorrow's "Maker."

6. The 3C Framework: Curiosity, Courage, Collaboration

Sustained creativity depends on a balance of mindset and behavior.

The 3C Framework offers a simple daily reminder of what fosters innovation in any environment.

- Curiosity: Ask questions without immediate judgment. Replace "That won't work" with "What would make it work?"
- Courage: Speak up with unconventional ideas and admit when you don't know.
- Collaboration: Co-create rather than compete; treat ideas as shared assets, not ownership stakes.

Team Ritual:

Start weekly meetings by highlighting one moment of curiosity, courage, or collaboration observed in the past week.

7. The Creativity Retrospective

Just as agile teams reflect on progress, creative teams should reflect on learning and mindset.

- Run a 30-minute session after a project or sprint:
- What ideas did we explore that surprised us?
- What risks did we take, and what did we learn from them?
- Where did our process feel most alive? Where did it feel stuck?
- What would we do differently next time?

Outcome:

A shared understanding of what conditions spark creativity, and how to intentionally recreate them.

8. Building a Culture of Everyday Experimentation

Frameworks and tools matter, but the real goal is to normalize creativity as an everyday act.

Encourage micro-experiments: five-minute brainstorms, visual thinking in meetings, cross-team pairings, or "idea-of-the-week" channels.

Remember:

Creativity doesn't live in big moments, it thrives in habits, rituals, and shared language. When teams are given permission to explore, challenge, and play, innovation becomes not an event, but a culture.

9. SCAMPER: A Tool for Creative Brainstorming

Sometimes, all you need to spark creativity is a structured prompt. SCAMPER is a technique that pushes teams to look at problems differently by asking targeted questions:

- Substitute: What can we replace to improve this?
- Combine: Can we merge two ideas into something new?
- Adapt: How can we tweak this to fit a different context?
- Modify: What can we change to make it better?
- Put to another use: Could this serve a completely different purpose?
- Eliminate: What can we remove to simplify it?
- Reverse: What happens if we flip this idea upside down?

SCAMPER encourages teams to break out of habitual thinking and explore fresh possibilities.

10. Psychological Safety: Creating a Safe Space for Risk-Taking

Teams can't innovate if they're afraid to fail. Psychological safety, the belief that it's okay to take risks, ask questions, and make mistakes, is the foundation of creative collaboration.

To foster psychological safety:
- Encourage experimentation and treat failure as a learning opportunity.
- Celebrate lessons learned, even when things don't go as planned.
- Show vulnerability as a leader—it sets the tone for openness and trust.

A safe team is a creative team.

11. Digital Tools for Collaborative Creativity

In today's world, creativity often happens across distances. Digital tools make it possible for teams to brainstorm, design, and collaborate in real time, no matter where they are. Some of my go-to platforms include:

- Miro and MURAL: Perfect for virtual brainstorming and visual mapping.
- Figma: A design tool that's great for prototyping and collaborative iteration.

- Notion: Ideal for organizing ideas, sharing notes, and keeping everyone on the same page.

These tools remove physical barriers, enabling creativity to flourish in hybrid or remote environments.

I'll say this a thousand more times, but creativity isn't a mystical talent reserved for a lucky few, it's a skill that teams can cultivate with the right tools and frameworks. Whether you're using design thinking to tackle a complex challenge, running a participatory workshop to bring stakeholders together, or creating a GIGA-map to visualize a system, the goal is the same: to unlock the potential that already exists within your team.

These strategies have been transformative in my own work, helping to turn big ideas into actionable solutions. They're not just about generating ideas, they're about building a culture where creativity becomes second nature. And in today's world, that's not just valuable, it's essential.

Chapter 12:
Imagining the Unknown

The morning holds a kind of magic that's hard to describe, a stillness where the mind feels unburdened by the weight of the day ahead. In those early hours, with a fresh cup of coffee in hand and the world just beginning to stir, anything seems possible. This is the time when the designer's mindset thrives and the entrepreneur's courage takes shape, a moment of quiet curiosity where the ordinary becomes extraordinary.

I was sitting by the ocean one morning, watching the waves gently rise and fall. The horizon stretched endlessly, an expanse of blue that seemed both infinite and intimate. I closed my eyes and imagined a world untouched by maps, where no one knew what lay beyond the sea. What would it be like to navigate without certainty, to see the world not as it is, but as it could be?

That moment reminded me of Fridtjof Nansen's bold expedition aboard the Fram—an audacious attempt to drift across the Arctic Ocean, guided not by precise charts but by trust in nature, science, and vision. In an age before GPS or satellite tracking, Nansen embraced the unknown, letting go of control and choosing to believe that forward motion could come from the forces around him—if only he dared to align with them.

That same spirit lives in the designer who rethinks how we solve problems, and in the entrepreneur who dares to build something from nothing. Both must navigate ambiguity. Both must strip away assumptions and imagine what doesn't yet exist. And both must ask the uncomfortable but vital questions that push the world forward.

As we close this book, I invite you to step into this mindset, not just as a designer or entrepreneur by title, but by thought. It's not about having all the answers. It's about seeing the possibility in small steps, about challenging the conventions that hold us back, and about daring, like Nansen, to ask, "What if?"

The Power of Starting Fresh and Imagining the Unknown

Picture a blank page. No lines, no edges, no restrictions, just endless potential. There's something both thrilling and terrifying about starting fresh, about standing at the edge of the unknown with nothing but your imagination to guide you. Designers know this feeling well; it's the beginning of every new project, every new idea, every new world they dream into existence.

Now, imagine walking through a dense forest at dawn, the kind where sunlight barely filters through the canopy, and the air hums with possibility. You can't see the path ahead, but you step forward anyway, guided by instinct and curiosity. This is what it means to imagine the unknown, to embrace the uncertainty of discovery, trusting that exploration will lead to something meaningful.

Starting fresh doesn't mean erasing the past; it means letting go of assumptions, habits, and the comfort of familiarity. It means viewing the world as a beginner again, questioning even the most obvious truths. What if roads weren't paved but grew organically? What if buildings adapted to the people inside them? What if the systems we live by today were redesigned for tomorrow's needs?

Imagining the unknown is about staying open to possibilities. It's about seeing potential where others see limits and allowing yourself to wander through ideas without a map. It's the willingness to sketch without worrying about straight lines, to write without worrying about perfect words, to build without worrying about perfect blueprints.

Starting fresh and imagining the unknown aren't just tools for designers, they're tools for anyone seeking change. Whether it's a new business, a new routine, or a new way of thinking, the act of starting fresh allows us to reimagine the world and our place in it. It's where transformation begins.

The Evolution of DDE in a Rapidly Changing World

In the coming decades, the boundaries between industries, disciplines, and markets will continue to blur. Entrepreneurs will need to act as connectors, bridging technology, design, and social impact to create holistic solutions. The evolution of DDE will reflect this need for integration, with several key trends shaping its trajectory:

1. The Era of Hyper-Personalization
As technology advances, businesses will move beyond one-size-fits-all solutions to create hyper-personalized products and services. DDE will guide entrepreneurs in designing experiences that respond to individual needs without sacrificing scalability.

2. The Rise of Collaborative Ecosystems
The future of entrepreneurship lies in networks, not silos. Startups will increasingly collaborate with other businesses, governments, and communities to co-create systemic solutions. DDE's emphasis on collaboration will be pivotal in building ecosystems that thrive on shared value.

3. From Product-Centric to Experience-Centric
Entrepreneurs will shift their focus from creating products to designing holistic

experiences. Whether it's a seamless digital platform or a socially impactful service, the experience will define success, and DDE will serve as the framework for crafting these transformative journeys.

The Role of Technology in Shaping DDE

Technology is not just a tool; it's a partner in design-driven entrepreneurship. From artificial intelligence to blockchain, the future will be defined by how entrepreneurs harness technology to amplify their impact.

1. AI-Driven Design

Artificial intelligence will revolutionize design by enabling real-time feedback, predictive analytics, and user-centric personalization. Entrepreneurs can leverage AI to test prototypes, analyze systems, and create solutions with unparalleled precision.

2. Blockchain for Transparency and Trust

Blockchain technology will become the backbone of ethical entrepreneurship. By ensuring transparency and accountability, it will help entrepreneurs build trust in industries where integrity is often questioned, such as supply chains and finance.

3. Augmented and Virtual Reality

AR and VR will blur the lines between the digital and physical worlds, enabling entrepreneurs to create immersive experiences. From virtual design studios to interactive product demos, these technologies will redefine how ideas are conceived and shared.

The Role of Sustainability in DDE

Sustainability is no longer optional, it's an imperative. Entrepreneurs who integrate sustainable practices into their business models will lead the way in addressing the world's most pressing environmental challenges.

1. Circular Economy Models

DDE will empower entrepreneurs to design circular business models that prioritize reuse, recycling, and resource efficiency. Products will be designed with their end-of-life in mind, creating value across their entire lifecycle.

2. Regenerative Design

Beyond sustainability lies regeneration, designing systems that actively restore and enhance the environment. Entrepreneurs will adopt regenerative principles to create ventures that give back more than they take.

3. Systemic Sustainability

DDE will expand sustainability beyond individual products or services to entire ecosystems. Entrepreneurs will use systemic design to address interconnected challenges, from reducing carbon footprints to fostering social equity.

The Role of Systemic Thinking in DDE

Systemic thinking will be the cornerstone of entrepreneurial success in the future. Entrepreneurs must learn to see the bigger picture, connecting dots across industries, geographies, and disciplines to create solutions that work at scale.

1. Complex Problem-Solving

As challenges grow more interconnected, entrepreneurs will need to embrace complexity rather than shy away from it. DDE's systemic approach will equip them to design interventions that consider every layer of the problem.

2. Multi-Stakeholder Engagement

The future of DDE will require engaging diverse stakeholders, from local communities to global policymakers. Entrepreneurs will need to design solutions that align the interests of all parties, fostering collaboration over competition.

3. Anticipating Second-Order Effects

Systemic thinking will help entrepreneurs foresee the ripple effects of their actions, avoiding unintended consequences and maximizing positive impact.

Exercise: The One-Minute Wild Idea

Take 60 seconds. Write down the most outrageous, impractical business idea you can think of—something wild, something impossible. Now, ask yourself:

What's one part of this idea that could work? Start there. Innovation begins when you dare to dream big, even if it's just for a minute.

Now, My Bold Ask: Think Like a Designer!

Look around you. Every object, every service, every process you encounter was designed by someone. But here's the secret: it doesn't mean it was designed perfectly. The chair you're sitting on could be more ergonomic. The apps on your phone could be more intuitive. Even the systems that govern society could be rethought to serve us better. Designers see these imperfections not as barriers, but as invitations to innovate.

Challenging conventions begins with questioning the default. Why are things done the way they are? What assumptions underlie the choices we take for granted? Designers step outside the comfort of "this is how it's always been" and venture into the possibility of "this is how it could be."

To think like a designer is to see the world as a work in progress—always evolving, always open to reimagination. You don't need to be a professional designer to embrace this mindset. Start small:

- Notice: Observe the patterns in your daily life and the systems around you. What works? What doesn't?
- Question: Ask yourself why things are the way they are. What would you change if you could?
- Experiment: Try new approaches, even if they seem unconventional. Small tweaks can lead to big shifts.

Believe that the progress is possible and that you have the power to go through it. It's about seeing the cracks in the foundation and knowing that with effort, imagination, and collaboration, those cracks can lead to something stronger, more beautiful, and better than what came before.

Change often feels daunting, like staring up at a towering mountain. But every mountain is climbed one step at a time.

Each sketch, prototype, or iteration is a small step forward. Each conversation, observation, or experiment adds to the momentum. What starts as a minor adjustment can ripple outward, shifting perspectives, improving lives, and reshaping systems. This is the quiet power of small steps: their ability to build on each other, to inspire action, and to spark meaningful change.

Consider the first electric lightbulb, the first personal computer, or the first vaccine. These weren't created in a single moment of brilliance but through countless incremental efforts, small tweaks, tiny failures, and relentless persistence. Each step mattered, even when it seemed insignificant in the moment.

The same is true in our daily lives. A single conversation can open the door to a new opportunity. A single decision can set a new course. A single act of courage can inspire others to follow. Small steps might feel inconsequential, but over time, they create momentum, they build confidence, and they lead to the kind of changes that once seemed impossible.

As you close this book, I encourage you to take one small step. Maybe it's questioning a convention you've always accepted. Maybe it's sketching out an idea that's been circling your mind. Maybe it's as simple as rethinking your morning routine. Whatever it is, take the step, no matter how small.

Because big changes don't start with grand gestures, they start with the willingness to begin. One step at a time, you have the power to design a better world. And that, perhaps, is the most extraordinary change of all.

Ending

I am a designer, and I am an entrepreneur, but beyond that, I am simply myself: someone committed to asking better questions, navigating uncertainty with intention, and creating space for others to do the same. Throughout this book, yes, the one you've impressively made it through, I spoke often of designers and entrepreneurs, and admittedly left out the inventors, engineers, researchers, artists, builders, and quiet thinkers who shape the world in equally powerful ways. But in the end, it's not about the labels we carry. It's about what we dare to imagine, what we choose to build, and who we allow ourselves to become.

But becoming isn't always elegant. It's rarely tidy. Our lives, specially for entrepreneurs, often look shiny from the outside, headlines about success, LinkedIn posts about milestones, the façade of momentum. But beneath it all, there's often a war raging inside, invisible to the world.

She wakes up each morning, puts on her best "I've got this" face, and walks into boardrooms, investor calls, and endless meetings, as if she isn't bleeding underneath from yesterday's rejection, today's uncertainty, and tomorrow's fear. Breaking down is a luxury she was never given, the company won't pause, the payroll won't wait, and the dream won't build itself.

She's the kind of founder who sits with her fears alone, quietly, in late-night offices after everyone's gone home. She overthinks every word in an investor pitch, every silence in a partnership negotiation, every customer that walks away. And yet, the next day, she shows up again, for her team, her clients, her vision, even when those same people have not always shown up for her.

She carries the scars of failures that burned, of doors slammed in her face, of people who told her "no" before they even understood what she was building. And yet she still carries the world in her hands as if it hasn't shattered her, as if she hasn't considered giving up a thousand times. People call her strong, but strength wasn't something she chose. It was survival. It was either keep building or watch the dream die.

Entrepreneurial strength is not glamor. It's burying pain so deeply that you can pitch with confidence even when you're terrified. It's forgetting what happiness looked like before the weight of responsibility became constant. It's learning to sit with exhaustion that no amount of sleep can fix, the kind that comes from carrying a vision too heavy for one person, and yet carrying it anyway.

And through it all, she doesn't complain. Because somewhere along the way, she learned the hardest truth of entrepreneurship: no one is coming to save her. The investors will doubt, the market will shift, the support system will waver. She is the rescue. The founder, the leader, the last line of defense between an idea and oblivion.

Perhaps the most frightening part is how good she has become at pretending she's fine. The practiced smile in interviews, the steady tone in investor updates, the calm presence in crisis meetings, when in truth, she's screaming behind her silence.

But here's the paradox: it's in that screaming silence, in that unseen battle, that real resilience is forged. Not the resilience of motivational posters, but the kind that keeps entire ventures alive. The kind that turns survival into innovation, exhaustion into breakthroughs, and silence into stories worth telling.

And maybe this is the truth behind the myth of "saving the world before breakfast." It's not about the brilliance of an idea or the glamour of overnight success. It's about the sleepless nights, the invisible battles, the quiet endurance that no one applauds. Because in the end, the world isn't saved in a moment of genius, it's saved, piece by piece, by those who keep showing up even when no one is watching.

The End.

Bibliography

This book draws from a wide range of inspirations and sources that have shaped its foundation and perspective on design thinking and systemic innovation. Key references include:

- Sevaldson, Birger. Designing Complexity: The Methodology and Practice of Systems Oriented Design. Common Ground Research Networks, 2022

- Brown, Tim. Change by Design: How Design Thinking Transforms Organizations and Inspires Innovation. HarperBusiness, 2009.

- Kelley, Tom & David Kelley. Creative Confidence: Unleashing the Creative Potential Within Us All. Crown Business, 2013.

- Liedtka, Jeanne & Tim Ogilvie. Designing for Growth: A Design Thinking Tool Kit for Managers. Columbia Business School Publishing, 2011.

- Norman, Donald A. The Design of Everyday Things. Revised and expanded edition. Basic Books, 2013.

- Martin, Roger L. The Design of Business: Why Design Thinking Is the Next Competitive Advantage. Harvard Business Press, 2009.

- Lewrick, Michael, Patrick Link & Larry Leifer. The Design Thinking Toolbox: A Guide to Mastering the Most Popular and Valuable Innovation Methods. Wiley, 2018.

- Boyd, Graham., Reardon, Jack. Rebuild: The Economy, Leadership, and You. United Kingdom: Evolutesix Books, 2020.

- Boyd, Graham., Reardon, Jack. The Ergodic Investor and Entrepreneur. N.p.: Evolutesix Books, 2023.

- Stickdorn, Marc, Markus Edgar Hormess, Adam Lawrence & Jakob Schneider. This is Service Design Doing: Applying Service Design Thinking in the Real World. O'Reilly Media, 2018.

The remainder are sources used are available in order of appearance:

1   Central Intelligence Agency. "Iran – The World Factbook." CIA, 2023. Available at: https://www.cia.gov/the-world-factbook/
(see the entry for Iran: total area 1,648,195 sq km).

2   United Nations Population Division. "World Population Prospects 2024: Online Edition" (data for Iran). Available at: https://data.un.org/
(see the population totals for Iran).

3   Brookings Institution. "The Iranian Revolution — A timeline of events." Brookings, 2016. [Online] Available at: https://www.brookings.edu/articles/the-iranian-revolution-a-timeline-of-events/

4   United States Census Bureau. "What Is a Small Business?" U.S. Census Bureau, 2021. Available at: https://www.census.gov/library/stories/2021/01/what-is-a-small-business.html

5   Ng, L. H. "Corporate Entrepreneurship: The Development of New Business Ideas

and Opportunities within Large and Established Corporations." Goodfellow Publishers, 2015. Available at: https://www.goodfellowpublishers.com/free_files/Chapter%20 6-f75896ab4ae78d6de2333426f72069ed.pdf

6   Corporate Finance Institute. "Scalability - Build a Business to Changing Markets." Corporate Finance Institute, 2024. Available at: https://corporatefinanceinstitute.com/resources/management/ scalability/

7   Martin, Roger L. and Sally Osberg. "Social Entrepreneurship: The Case for Definition." Stanford Social Innovation Review, Winter 2007. Available at: https://ssir.org/articles/entry/social_ entrepreneurship_the_case_for_definition

8   MIT Sloan School of Management. "Intrapreneurship, explained." MIT Sloan, 2018. Available at: https://mitsloan.mit.edu/ideas-made-to-matter/intrapreneurship-explained

9   The Guardian. "Nokia: the rise and fall of a mobile phone giant." The Guardian, 3 Sep 2013. Available at: https://www.theguardian.com/technology/2013/sep/03/nokia-rise-fall-mobile-phone-giant

Lonely Entrepreneur. "5 Types of Entrepreneurs Defined & Explained: The Hustler Entrepreneur." Lonely Entrepreneur, 2023. Available at: https://lonelyentrepreneur.com/types-of-entrepreneurs/

10   Ellis, Natalie. "Growing BossBabe to a $20M Community." Kajabi Creator Stories. Available at: https://kajabi.com/creator-stories/natalie-ellis

11   EntrepreneursData. "Imitative Entrepreneurship: Meaning, Characteristics & Examples." EntrepreneursData, 2024. Available at: https://www.entrepreneursdata.com/imitative-entrepreneurship-meaning/

12   Reuters. "Iran's Snapp! App Dominates Ride-Hailing Market amid Tight Regulations." Reuters, 2023. Available at: https://www.reuters.com/technology/irans-snapp-app-dominates-ride-hailing-market-amid-tight-regulations-2023-02-15/

13   "11 Good Reasons to Buy an Existing Business." Walton College, University of Arkansas, Jan 15 2019. Available at: https://walton.uark.edu/insights/confessions-buying-an-existing-business.php

14   "The Mittelstand will redeem German innovation." The Economist, 14 Sept 2023. Available at: https://www.economist.com/business/2023/09/14/the-mittelstand-will-redeem-german-innovation/

15   Sharena Fabrika. "The History of Pottery and Ceramics: A Journey Through the Millennia." Sharena Fabrika, 2023. Available at: https://www.sharenafabrika.com/en/post/the-history-of-pottery-and-ceramics-a-journey-through-the-millennia

16   The Coca-Cola Company. "I'd Like to Buy the World a Coke." The Coca-Cola Company, 2024. Available at: https://www.coca-colacompany.com/about-us/history/id-like-to-buy-the-world-a-coke

17   The Metropolitan Museum of Art. "The Bauhaus, 1919-1933." The Metropolitan Museum of Art, 2015. Available at: https://www.metmuseum.org/essays/the-bauhaus-1919-1933/

18   Britannica. "International Style, Architecture." Britannica, 2025. Available at: https://www.britannica.com/art/International-Style-architecture

19   Smashing Magazine, 2011. Available at: https://www.smashingmagazine.com/2011/06/the-story-of-scandinavian-design-combining-function-and-aesthetics/

20   Klotz, Heinrich. The History of Postmodern Architecture. MIT Press, 1988. Available at: https://www.mitpress.mit.edu/9780262610674/the-history-of-postmodern-architecture/

21   HBS Online. "What is Human-Centered Design?" HBS Online Blog, 2020. Available at: https://online.hbs.edu/blog/post/what-is-human-centered-design

22   Yu, et al. "Thirty Years of Design for Sustainability: An Evolution of Research, Policy and Practice." Design Science, 2019. Available at: https://www.cambridge.org/core/journals/design-science/article/thirty-years-of-design-for-sustainability-an-evolution-of-research-policy-and-practice/826F8D B495185EB0AAF6118048A100C9

23   Brown, T. (2008). Design Thinking. Harvard Business Review, 86(6), 84–92. Retrieved from https://pubmed.ncbi.nlm.nih.gov/18605031

24   High Tech High. "What Is PBL?" High Tech High Graduate School of Education. Accessed November 4, 2025. https://hthgse.edu/what-is-pbl/

25   MindLab (Denmark) –

MindLab. "MindLab 2002-2018: How the legacy lives on." Apolitical, 18 Nov. 2019. https://apolitical.co/solution-articles/en/mindlab-2002-2018-how-the-legacy-lives-on

26   Zebras Unite. "Zebras Unite: Creating the Culture, Capital & Community for the Next Economy." Zebras Unite Co-Op, 2017. https://www.zebrasunite.coop/

27   How Spotify uses design to make personalization features delightful." Spotify Newsroom, 18 Oct 2023. Available at: https://newsroom.spotify.com/2023-10-18/how-spotify-uses-design-to-make-personalization-features-delightful/

28   Forsman & Bodenfors. "Changing How People Think of Milk." Forsman & Bodenfors, 2025. Available at: https://www.forsman.com/work/oatly/

29   UI/UX Development Using Figma based on Inclusive Design." Journal of Information & Visualization, 2023, 4(2): 227–234. Available at: https://www.researchgate.net/publication/389507410_UIUX_Development_Using_Figma_based_on_Inclusive_Design

30   Strate Design School. "Airbnb's Successful Design Thinking Story." Strate, 2023. Available at: https://strate.in/airbnbs-successful-design-thinking-story/

31   Porsche AG. "A brief history of the Porsche 911." Porsche.com, 14 June 2023. Available at: https://www.porsche.com/stories/innovation/a-brief-history-of-the-porsche-911/

32   Blakely, Sara. "How I Built Spanx from $5,000 and an Idea." Inc., 20 Jan 2012. Available at: https://www.inc.com/sara-blakely/how-sara-blakley-started-spanx.html

33   Wired. "Airbnb's Surprising Path to Y Combinator." Wired, Feb 21 2017. Available at: https://www.wired.com/2017/02/airbnbs-surprising-path-to-y-combinator/

34   Paumgarten, Nick. "Patagonia's Philosopher-King." The New Yorker, Sept. 19 2016. Available at: https://www.newyorker.com/magazine/2016/09/19/patagonias-philosopher-king

35   Mailchimp. "Mailchimp Sells for $12 Billion: The Largest Bootstrapped Exit Ever." TinySeed, 2021. Available at: https://tinyseed.com/latest/the-biggest-bootstrap-exit-ever-mailchimp-sells-for-12b

36   Silicon Valley's $400 Juicer May Be Feeling the Squeeze." Bloomberg, 19 Apr 2017. Available at: https://www.bloomberg.com/news/features/2017-04-19/silicon-valley-s-400-juicer-may-be-feeling-the-squeeze

37   "They built it, but people did not come: the cautionary tale of Quibi." The Guardian, 23 Oct 2020. Available at: https://www.theguardian.com/tv-and-radio/2020/oct/23/why-quibi-is-a-cautionary-tale-shortform-netflix

38   Corporate Adolescence: Why Did 'We' Not Work?" Texas Law Review, 2021. Available at:

https://texaslawreview.org/corporate-adolescence-why-did-we-not-work/

39   STATION F. "About – STATION F." STATION F, 2025. Available at: https://stationf.co/about

40   Changing Experiences through Empathy – The Adventure Series." ThisIsDesignThinking.net. December 2014. Accessed November 4, 2025. https://thisisdesignthinking.net/2014/12/changing-experiences-through-empathy-ge-healthcares-adventure-series/

41   Bank of America. "Keep the Change® Savings Program." Bank of America. Accessed November 4 2025. https://www.bankofamerica.com/deposits/keep-the-change/

42   World Bank. "Mobile Payments Go Viral: M-PESA in Kenya." Working Paper No. 54338, November 2010.
https://documents1.worldbank.org/curated/en/638851468048259219/pdf/543380WP0M1PES1BOX0349405B01PUBLIC1.pdf

43   Smith, Andrea Nagy; Canales, Rodrigo; Drenttel, William; Elias, Jaan. Design at Mayo: Case Study 09-034. Yale School of Management, November 2010. "The Founding of SPARC" section. https://cases.som.yale.edu/design-mayo/founding-sparc/founding-sparc

44   Interface, Inc. "Mission Zero: Lessons for the Future." Interface, 2018. Available at: https://www.interface.com/content/dam/interfaceinc/interface/sustainability/emea/25th-anniversary-report/Interface_MissionZeroCel_Booklet_EN.pdf

45   Too Good To Go. "About Us" (Copenhagen, Denmark: Too Good To Go A/S, 2016). https://www.toogoodtogo.com/en-us/about-us/

46   "M-KOPA Solar: The Pay-As-You-Go model." Engineering for Change, "M-KOPA IV Solar Home System". https://www.engineeringforchange.org/solutions/product/m-kopa-iv-solar-home-system/

47   Patagonia. "Don't Buy This Jacket, Black Friday and The New York Times." Patagonia Stories, 25 Nov 2011. Available at: https://www.patagonia.com/stories/dont-buy-this-jacket-black-friday-and-the-new-york-times/story-18615.html

48   Wood, Johnny. "Reuse rather than recycle packaging: TerraCycle CEO Tom Szaky." World Economic Forum, 2023. https://www.weforum.org/stories/2023/10/reuse-packaging-loop-zero-waste-terracycle-tom-szaky/

49   Agència de Salut Pública de Barcelona (ASPB), GREAF & CESS. "Results Report: Salut als Carrers (Health in the Streets) – Superblocks in Barcelona". Barcelona: ASPB, 2021. https://www.aspb.cat/wp-content/uploads/2021/10/English-ASPB_salut-carrers-resultsreport-Superblocks.pdf

50   Allchin, Josie. "Putting the 'we' into Wii: Tech names make themselves more family friendly." Marketing Week, 2 March 2011. Available at:
https://www.marketingweek.com/putting-the-we-into-wii-tech-names-make-themselves-more-family-friendly/

51   Visnic, Bill. "Ford's Dedicated Interior Ergonomics Appeal to All Demographics." Ward's Auto, 6 June 2007. Available at: https://wardsauto.com/news/archive-wards-ford-dedicated-interior-ergonomics-appeal-to-all-demographics/770761/

52   Blakely, Sara. 2012. "How Sara Blakely of Spanx Turned $5,000 Into $1 Billion." Forbes, March 26. https://www.forbes.com/global/2012/0326/billionaires-12-feature-united-states-spanx-sara-blakely-american-booty.html

53   Nooyi, Indra. "Companies Can Be a Force for Good: How PepsiCo's 'Performance with Purpose' Strategy Drove Growth and Sustainability." Duke University Fuqua School of Business Dialogue Project, October 2014. https://www.fuqua.duke.edu/dialogue-project-duke/indra-nooyi-companies-can-be-force-good

54   Womens Agenda. "Bumble's IPO Makes Whitney Wolfe Herd a Billionaire, and Youngest Woman to Take a Tech Unicorn Public." Womens Agenda, February 11, 2021. https://womensagenda.com.au/business/bumbles-ipo-makes-whitney-wolfe-herd-a-billionaire-and-youngest-woman-to-take-a-tech-unicorn-public/

55   Brown, B., Shibuya, A., & Ter Wengel, M. "Women-Led Startups Received Just 2.3 % of VC Funding in 2020." Harvard Business Review, 25 Feb. 2021. https://hbr.org/2021/02/women-led-startups-received-just-2-3-of-vc-funding-in-2020

56   The LEGO Group. "Children Are Our Role Models": Child Participation Through Culture, Co-creation and Inspiring Change. Billund, Denmark: The LEGO Group, 2022. https://www.kidsincluded.report/the-lego-group

57   Slack. "Beyond the smile: how emoji use has evolved in the workplace." Slack, 13 July 2022. Available at: https://slack.com/blog/collaboration/emoji-use-at-work